Modeling Bounded Rationality

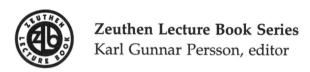 **Zeuthen Lecture Book Series**
Karl Gunnar Persson, editor

Modeling Bounded Rationality, Ariel Rubinstein

Modeling Bounded Rationality

Ariel Rubinstein

The MIT Press
Cambridge, Massachusetts
London, England

Second printing, 1998

© 1998 Massachusetts Institute of Technology

This book was set in Palatino using Ventura Publisher under Windows 95 by Wellington Graphics.

Printed and bound in the United States of America.

Library of Congress Cataloging-in-Publication Data

Rubinstein, Ariel.
  Modeling bounded rationality / Ariel Rubinstein.
    p. cm. — (Zeuthen lecture book series)
  Includes bibliographical references (p.) and index.
  ISBN 0-262-18187-8 (hardcover : alk. paper). — ISBN 0-262-68100-5 (pbk. : alk. paper)
    1. Decision-making. 2. Economic man. 3. Game theory. 4. Rational expectations (Economic theory) I. Title. II. Series.
HD30.23.R83 1998   97-40481
153.8'3—dc21   CIP

Contents

Series Foreword

The Zeuthen Lectures offer a forum for leading scholars to develop and synthesize novel results in theoretical and applied economics. They aim to present advances in knowledge in a form accessible to a wide audience of economists and advanced students of economics. The choice of topics will range from abstract theorizing to economic history. Regardless of the topic, the emphasis in the lecture series will be on originality and relevance. The Zeuthen Lectures are organized by the Institute of Economics, University of Copenhagen.

The lecture series is named after Frederik Zeuthen, a former professor at the Institute of Economics, and it is only appropriate that the first Zeuthen lecturer is Ariel Rubinstein, who has refined and developed a research program to which Frederik Zeuthen made important initial contributions.

Karl Gunnar Persson

Preface

This book is a collection of notes I have developed over the last eight years and presented in courses and lectures at the London School of Economics (1989), Hebrew University (1989), University of Pennsylvania (1990), Columbia University (1991), Princeton University (1992, 1995), University of Oslo (1994), Paris X (1995), Oberwesel (1995), New York University (1996), and my home university, Tel Aviv (1990, 1994). I completed writing the book while I was a visiting scholar at the Russell Sage Foundation, New York. A preliminary version was presented as the Core Lectures at Louvain-La-Neuve in October 1995; this version served as the basis for my Zeuthen Lectures at the University of Copenhagen in December 1996.

The book provides potential material for a one-term graduate course. The choice of material is highly subjective. Bibliographic notes appear at the end of each chapter. The projects that follow those notes contain speculative material and ideas that the reader should consider with caution.

My thanks to my friends Bart Lipman and Martin Osborne for their detailed comments and encouragement. I am grateful to all those students, especially Dana Heller, Rani Spigeler, and Ehud Yampuler, who commented on drafts of several chapters, to Nina Reshef, who helped edit the English-language manuscript, to Dana Heller, who prepared the index, and to Gregory McNamee who copyedited the manuscript.

Introduction

1 "Modeling" and "Bounded Rationality"

The series of lectures that constitute the chapters in this book concerns *modeling bounded rationality*. The choice of the title "modeling bounded rationality" rather than "models of bounded rationality" or "economic models of bounded rationality" emphasizes that the focus is not on substantive conclusions derived from the models but on the tools themselves. As to the term *bounded rationality*, putting fences around a field is often viewed as a picky activity. Nonetheless, it is important in this case in that the term has been used in many ways, sometimes just to say that we deal with incomplete (or bad) models. Lying within the domain of this investigation are models in which elements of the process of choice are embedded explicitly. Usually, economic models do not spell out the procedures by which decisions of the economic units are made; here, we are interested in models in which procedural aspects of decision making are explicitly included.

I will not touch the growing literature on *evolutionary economics* for three reasons. First, the topic of evolutionary/learning models deserves a complete and separate series of lectures. Second, the mathematical methods involved in models of evolutionary economics are quite different than those used here. Third, and most important, I want to place an admittedly vague dividing line between the two bodies of research. Within the scope of our discussion, I wish to include models in which decision makers make *deliberate* decisions by applying procedures that guide their reasoning about "what" to do, and probably also about "how" to decide. In contrast, evolutionary models treat agents as automata, merely responding to changing environments, *without deliberating* about their decisions.

2 The Aim of This Book

The basic motivation for studying models of bounded rationality springs from our dissatisfaction with the models that adhere to the "perfect rational man" paradigm. This dissatisfaction results from the strong tension arising from a comparison of the assumptions made by economic modelers about "perfect rationality" with observations about human behavior. This situation would be much less disturbing if we were able to perceive microeconomic models as "miraculous machines" that produce empirical linkages between economic parameters. I doubt that this is the case. I adhere to the view that the main objective of economic theory is to deduce interesting relationships between concepts that appear in our reasoning on interactive situations. Adopting this approach makes it important to examine the plausibility of the assumptions, and not only the conclusions.

The emphasis on the modeling process, rather than on the substance, does not diminish the importance of the goal, which is to construct models that will be useful tools in providing explanations of economic (or other) phenomena that could not otherwise be explained (ideally comparable to results such as those achieved by Spence's signaling model). The following are *examples* of basic intuitions that await proper explanation:

• Advertising is an activity that is supposed to influence an economic agent's decisions not only by supplying information and changing preferences, but also by influencing the way decisions are made.

• Decision makers are not equally capable of analyzing a situation even when the information available to all of them is the same. The differences in their economic success can be attributed to these differences.

• Many social institutions, like standard contracts and legal procedures, exist, or are structured as they are, in order to simplify decision making.

3 The State of the Art

Dissatisfaction with classical theory and attempts to replace the basic model of rational man with alternative decision models are not new. Ideas of how to model bounded rationality have been lurking in the economics literature for many years. Papers written by Herbert Simon as early as the mid-1950s have inspired many proposals in this vein. Although Simon received worldwide recognition for his work, only recently has his call affected mainstream economic theory. Only a few of the modeling tools we will discuss here have been applied to economic settings. What is more, the usefulness of these models is still far from being established. In fact, I have the impression that many of us feel that the attempts to model bounded rationality have yet to find the right track. It is difficult to pinpoint any economic work not based on fully rational microeconomic behavior that yields results as rich, deep, and interesting as those achieved by standard models assuming full rationality.

I consider these to be the three fundamental obstacles we have to overcome:

• The construction of pertinent new theories of choice. We have clear, casual, and experimental observations that indicate systematic deviations from the rational man paradigm. We look for models that will capture this evidence.

• The refinement of the notion of choice. Decision makers also make decisions about how and when to decide; we look for models that will relate to such decisions as well.

• The transformation of the notion of equilibrium. Current solution concepts, especially those concerning strategic interactions and rational expectations, are based on an implicit assumption that individuals know the prevailing equilibrium. But decision makers also have to make inferences about the environment in which they operate, an activity dependent on their ability to analyze the situation. We look for models in which the making of inferences will be the basic activity occupying the decision maker.

The evaluation that very little has been achieved makes one wonder whether it is at all possible to construct interesting models without the assumption of substantive rationality. Is there something fundamental that prevents us from constructing useful bounded rationality models, or have we been "brainwashed" by our conventional models? One intriguing idea is that substantive rationality is actually a constraint on the *modeler* rather than an assumption about the real world. The rationality of the decision maker can be seen as the minimal discipline to be imposed on the modeler. Our departure from the rational man paradigm represents a removal of those chains. However, there are an infinite number of "plausible" models that can explain social phenomena; without such chains we are left with a strong sense of arbitrariness. Although I have nothing to contribute to the discussion of this issue, I think it is worth mentioning.

In any case, even if one believes like Kenneth Arrow (1987), that "there is no general principle that prevents the creation of an economic theory based on other hypotheses than that of rationality," the only way to prove the power of including the procedural aspects of decision making in specific economic theories is by actually doing so. This is the challenge for scholars of "bounded rationality."

4 A Personal Note

This book is not intended to be a triumphal march of a field of research but a journey into the dilemmas faced by economic theorists attempting to expand the scope of the theory in the direction of bounded rationality. Some of the ideas I discuss are only just evolving.

By choosing such a topic for this series of lectures, I am taking the risk that my presentation will be less clear, less persuasive, and much more speculative than if I were discussing a more established topic. However, these attributes can also be advantageous, especially to the students among the readers. Newcomers to economic theory are in the best position to pursue themes that require imagination and invention. Students have a major advantage over us teachers in that, they are not (yet) indoctrinated by the body of literature so firmly rooted in the notion of rational man.

Finally, within the wide borders I have tried to draw, the selection of material is strongly biased toward topics with which I have been personally involved, either as an author or as an interested observer. I have not tried to be objective in the choice of topics, nor have I tried to summarize views held by "the profession." In this respect, the book is personal and aims at presenting my own views and knowledge of the subject.

5 Bibliographic Notes

Some of the methodological issues regarding the construction of new models on hypotheses other than that of rationality are discussed in Hogarth and Reder (1987). In particular, the reader is encouraged to review the four articles by Arrow, Lucas, Thaler, and Tversky and Kahneman.

Selten (1989) proposes an alternative view of bounded rationality and provides an overview of some of the issues discussed up to the late 1980s. For other views on modeling rational and bounded-rational players, see Binmore (1987, 1988) and Aumann (1996). Lipman (1995a) contains a short survey covering some of the topics discussed in this book.

1   Bounded Rationality in Choice

1.1   The "Rational Man"

In economic theory, a rational decision maker is an agent who has to choose an alternative after a process of deliberation in which he answers three questions:

- "What is feasible?"
- "What is desirable?"
- "What is the best alternative according to the notion of desirability, given the feasibility constraints?"

This description lacks any predictive power regarding a single decision problem, inasmuch as one can always explain the choice of an alternative, from a given set, as an outcome of a process of deliberation in which that outcome is indeed considered the best. Herein lies a key assumption regarding the rational man: The operation of discovering the feasible alternatives and the operation of defining the preferences are entirely independent. That is, if the decision maker ranks one alternative above another when facing a set of options that includes both, he will rank them identically when encountering any other decision problem in which these two alternatives are available.

Formally, the most abstract model of choice refers to a decision maker who faces choices from sets of alternatives that are subsets of some "grand set" **A**. A *choice problem*, A, is a subset of **A**; the task of the decision maker is to single out one element of A.

To conclude, the scheme of the choice procedure employed by the rational decision maker is as follows:

(P-1) *The rational man*   The primitive of the procedure is a preference relation $\succsim$ over a set **A**. Given a choice problem $A \subseteq$ **A**, choose an element x^* in A that is $\succsim$-optimal (that is, $x^* \succsim x$ for all $x \in A$).

For simplicity, it will be assumed through the rest of this chapter that preferences are asymmetric (i.e., if $a \succsim b$ then not $b \succsim a$). Thus, the decision maker has in mind a preference relation, $\succsim$, over the set of alternatives **A**. Facing a problem A, the decision maker chooses an element in the set A, denoted by $C_{\succsim}(A)$, satisfying $C_{\succsim}(A) \succsim x$ for all $x \in A$. Sometimes we replace the preference relation with a utility function, $u: \mathbf{A} \to \mathbf{R}$, with the understanding that $u(a) \geq u(a')$ is equivalent to $a \succsim a'$. (Of course, some assumptions are needed for establishing the equivalence between the existence of preferences and the existence of a utility function).

Let us uncover some of the assumptions buried in the rational man procedure:

• *Knowledge of the problem*   The decision maker has a clear picture of the choice problem he faces: he is fully aware of the set of alternatives from which he has to choose (facing the problem A, the decision maker can choose any $x \in A$, and the chosen x^* cannot be less preferred than any other $x \in A$). He neither invents nor discovers new courses of actions (the chosen x^* cannot be outside the set A).

• *Clear preferences*   The decision maker has a complete ordering over the entire set of alternatives.

• *Ability to optimize*   The decision maker has the skill necessary to make whatever complicated calculations are needed to discover his optimal course of action. His ability to calculate is unlimited, and he does not make mistakes. (The simplicity of the formula "$\max_{a \in A} u(a)$" is misleading; the operation may, of course, be very complex.)

• *Indifference to logically equivalent descriptions of alternatives and choice sets* The choice is invariant to logically equivalent changes of descriptions of alternatives. That is, replacing one "alternative" with another "alternative" that is "logically equivalent" does not affect the choice. If the sets A and B are equal, then the choice from A is the same as the choice from B.

Comment Often the preferences on a set of alternatives are derived from a more detailed structure. For example, it is often the case that the decision maker bases his preferences, defined on **A**, on the *calculation of consequences* yielded from **A**. That is, he perceives a set of possible consequences, **C**. He has a preference relation over **C** (probably represented by a numerical function, $V: \mathbf{C} \to \mathbf{R}$). He perceives the causal dependence of a consequence on a chosen alternative, described by a *consequence function*, $f: \mathbf{A} \to \mathbf{C}$. He then chooses, from any set $A \subseteq \mathbf{A}$, the alternative in A that yields the best consequence—that is, he solves the optimization problem $\max_{a \in A} V(f(a))$. In other words, the preference relation on **A** is induced from the composition of the consequence function and the preference relation on **C**.

In order to deal with the situation in which the decision maker assumes that the connection between the action and the consequence has elements of uncertainty, we usually enrich the model. A space of states, Ω, is added. One element of Ω represents the list of exogenous factors that are relevant to the decision maker's interests and are beyond his control. The consequence function is taken to depend on Ω as well; that is, $f: \mathbf{A} \times \Omega \to \mathbf{C}$. Each action $a \in \mathbf{A}$ corresponds to an "act" (a function that specifies an element in **C** for each state in Ω) $a(\omega) = f(a, \omega)$. The preference relation on **A** is induced from a preference on "acts." A choice problem now is a pair (A, Ω) where $A \subseteq \mathbf{A}$ is the set of alternatives, whereas $\Omega \subseteq \mathbf{\Omega}$ is the set of states not excluded by the information the decision maker receives. Usually, it is taken that the rational man's choice is based on a belief on the set $\mathbf{\Omega}$, a belief he updates by the Bayesian formula whenever he is informed that an event $\Omega \subseteq \mathbf{\Omega}$ happens.

Note that underlying this structure, both with and without uncertainty, is the assumption that the decision maker clearly perceives the action–consequence relationship.

1.2 The Traditional Economist's Position

Economists have often been apologetic about the assumption that decision makers behave like the "rational man." Introspection suggests that those assumptions are often unrealistic. This is probably the reason why economists argued long ago that the rational man paradigm has to be taken less literally.

The "traditional" argument is roughly this: In economics, we are mainly interested in the *behavior* of the decision maker and not in the process leading to his decision. Even if the decision maker does not behave in the manner described by the rational man procedure, it still may be the case that his behavior can be described *as if* he follows such a procedure. This is sufficient for the purpose of economics.

A good demonstration of this "as if" idea is given in consumer theory. Imagine a consumer who operates in a world with two goods, 1 and 2, who has budget I, and who faces prices p_1 and p_2. Assume that the consumer allocates the fraction α of his income to good 1 and $(1 - \alpha)$ of the income to good 2 (for every I, p_1 and p_2). This behavior rule may be the result of activating a rule of thumb. Nonetheless, it may still be presented as if it is the outcome of the consumer's maximization of the utility function $x_1^\alpha x_2^{1-\alpha}$.

Let us return to the general framework. The following argument was designed to support the traditional point of view. Consider a decision maker whose behavior regarding choices from subsets of the set **A** is described by a function C whose domain is the set of all non-empty subsets of **A** and whose range is the set **A**. The element $C(A)$ is interpreted as the decision maker's choice whenever he confronts the decision problem A. For every A, $C(A) \in A$. (Note that for simplicity, and in contrast to some of the literature, it is required here that $C(A)$ is a single element in A and not a subset of A).

We now come to an important necessary and sufficient condition for a choice function to be induced by a decision maker who behaves like a rational man. It is said that the decision maker's behavior function C satisfies the *consistency* condition (sometimes referred to as the "independence of irrelevant alternatives") if for all $A_1 \subseteq A_2 \subseteq A$, if $C(A_2) \in A_1$ then $C(A_1) = C(A_2)$. That is, if the element chosen from the large set (A_2) is a member of the smaller set (A_1), then the decision maker chooses this element from the smaller set as well. It is easy to see that C is consistent if and only if there exists a preference relation $\succsim$ over **A** such that for all $A \subseteq A$, $C(A)$ is the $\succsim$-maximal element in A.

Proof Of course, if for every subset A the element $C(A)$ is the $\succsim$-maximal element in A, then the choice function C satisfies the consistency condition. Assume that C satisfies the consistency condition. Define a preference relation $\succsim$ by $a \succsim b$ if $a = C(\{a, b\})$. We first verify that $\succsim$ is transitive. If $a \succsim b$ and $b \succsim c$, then $a = C(\{a, b\})$ and $b = C(\{b, c\})$. Then $C(\{a, b, c\}) = a$; otherwise, the consistency condition is violated with respect to one of the sets, $\{a, b\}$ or $\{b, c\}$. Therefore, by the consistency condition, $C(\{a, c\}) = a$; that is, $a \succsim c$. To verify that for every set A, $C(A)$ is the $\succsim$-maximal element in A, notice that for any element $a \in A$, $\{a, C(A)\} \subseteq A$ and because C satisfies the consistency condition, $C(\{a, C(A)\}) = C(A)$, therefore by definition of $\succsim$, $C(A) \succsim a$.

The conclusion from this simple analysis is that choice functions that satisfy the consistency condition, even if they are not derived from a rational man procedure, can be described *as if* they are derived by some rational man. The significance of this result depends on the existence of plausible procedures that satisfy the consistency condition even though they do not belong to the scheme (P-1) of choosing a maximal element. One such classic example is what Simon termed the *satisficing procedure:*

(P-2)   The primitives of the procedure are O, an ordering of the set **A**, and a set $S \subseteq \mathbf{A}$ (as well as a tie-breaking rule; see below). For any decision problem A, sequentially examine the alternatives in A, according to the ordering O, until you confront an alternative that is a member of the set S, the set of "satisfactory" alternatives. Once you find such an element, stop and choose it. For the case where no element of A belongs to S, use the tie-breaking rule that satisfies the consistency requirement (such as choosing the last element in A).

Any procedure within the scheme (P-2) satisfies the consistency condition. To verify this, suppose that $A_1 \subseteq A_2$ and $C(A_2) \in A_1$, that is, $C(A_2)$ is the first (according to the ordering O) satisfactory alternative in A_2, then it is also the first satisfactory alternative in the subset A_1. If $C(A_2) \notin S$, then A_1 also does not include any element belonging to S, and because the tie-breaking rule satisfies the consistency condition, we have $C(A_2) = C(A_1)$.

A special case of (P-2) is one where the set S is derived from two parameters, a function V and a number v^*, so that $S = \{a \in \mathbf{A} \mid V(a) \geq v^*\}$. The function V assigns a number to each of the potential alternatives, whereas v^* is the aspiration level. The decision maker searches for an alternative that satisfies the condition that its value be above the aspiration level. For example, in the "finding a worker" problem, the set of alternatives is the set of candidates for a job, the ordering might be the alphabetical ordering of the candidates' names or an enumeration of their social security numbers, $V(a)$ may be the grade that candidate a gets in a test, and v^* is the required minimal grade. Note that instead of having a maximization problem, "$\max_{a \in A} V(a)$," the decision maker who follows (P-2) solves what seems to be a simpler problem: "Find an $a \in A$ for which $V(a) \geq v^*$."

1.3 The Attack on the Traditional Approach

The fact that we have found a family of plausible procedures that are not similar to the rational man procedure yet consistent with rationality provides support for the traditional economic position. However, the problem with this position is that it is difficult to propose *additional* procedures for inducing consistent choice functions.

To appreciate the difficulties in finding such examples, note that in (P-2) the ordering in which the alternatives are examined is fixed independent of the particular choice set. However, if the ordering by which the alternatives are examined is dependent on the set, a clash with the consistency condition arises. Consider the following decision procedure scheme:

(P-3) The primitives of the procedure are two different orderings of **A**, O_1 and O_2, a natural number n^*, and a set S (plus a tie-breaking rule). For a choice problem A, employ (P-2) with the ordering O_1 if the number of elements in A is below n^* and with O_2 if the number of alternatives in A is above n^*.

It is easy to see that a procedure within the scheme (P-3) will often not satisfy the consistency condition. The fact that an element is the first element, by the ordering O_2, belonging to S in a "large" set A_2 does not guarantee that it is the first, by the other ordering O_1, belonging to S in a "smaller" subset A_1.

In the rest of this section, we will refer to three motives often underlying procedures of choice that may conflict with the rational man paradigm: "framing effects," the "tendency to simplify problems," and the "search for reasons." In the next section, we present evidence from the psychological literature that confirms that these motives systematically appear in human choice situations.

Framing Effects

By framing effects, we refer to phenomena rooted solely in the way that the decision problem is framed, not in the content of the choice problem. Recall that a choice problem is defined as a choice of an element from a *set*. In practice, this set has to be described; the way that it is described may affect the choice. For example, the model does not allow distinct choices between the lists of alternatives (a, b, b) and (a, a, a, b, b) because the sets $\{a, b, b\}$ and $\{a, a, a, b, b\}$ are identical. If, however, the language in which the sets are specified is a language of "lists," then the following procedural scheme is well defined:

(P-4) Choose the alternative that appears in the list most often (and apply some rule that satisfies the consistency condition for tie-breaking).

Of course, such a procedure does not satisfy the consistency condition. It does not even induce a well-defined choice function.

The Tendency to Simplify Decision Problems

Decision makers tend to simplify choice problems, probably as a method of saving deliberation resources. An example of a procedure motivated by the simplification effort is the following:

(P-5) The primitives of the procedure are an ordering O and a preference relation $\succeq$ on the set $\mathbf{A}$. Given a decision problem A, pick the first and last elements (by the ordering O) among the set A and choose the better alternative (by the preference relation $\succeq$) between the two.

In this case, the decision maker does not consider all the elements in A but only those selected by a predetermined rule. From this sample, he then chooses the $\gtrsim$-best alternative. If the alternatives are a, b, and c, the preference ranking is $b > a > c$, and the ordering O is alphabetical, then the alternative a will be chosen from among $\{a, b, c\}$ and b from among $\{a, b\}$, a choice conflicting with the consistency condition. (Try to verify the plausibility of this procedural motive by examining the method by which you make a choice from a large catalog.)

The Search for Reasons
Choices are often made on the basis of reasons. If the reasons are independent of the choice problem, the fact that the decision maker is motivated by them does not cause any conflict with rationality. Sometimes, however, the reasons are "internal," that is, dependent on the decision problem; in such a case, conflict with rationality is often unavoidable. For example, in the next scheme of decision procedures, the decision maker has in mind a *partial* ordering, D, defined on **A**. The interpretation given to $a\ D\ b$ is that a "clearly dominates" b. Given a decision problem, A, the decision maker selects an alternative that dominates over more alternatives than does any other alternative in the set A.

(P-6) The primitive is a partial ordering D. Given a problem A, for each alternative $a \in A$, count the number $N(a)$ of alternatives in A that are dominated (according to the partial ordering D). Select the alternative a^* so that $N(a^*) \geq N(a)$ for all $a \in A$ (and use a rule that satisfies the consistency requirement for tie-breaking).

By (P-6) a reason for choosing an alternative is the "large number of alternatives dominated by the chosen alternative." This is an "internal reason" in the sense that the preference of one alternative over another is determined by the other elements in the set. Of course, (P-6) often does not satisfy the consistency condition.

1.4 Experimental Evidence

Economic theory relies heavily on intuitions and casual observations of real life. However, despite being an economic theorist who
rarely approaches data, I have to agree that an understanding of
the procedural aspects of decision making should rest on an empirical or experimental exploration of the algorithms of decision.
Too many routes diverge from the rational man paradigm, and the
input of experimentation may offer some guides for moving
onward.

The refutation of the rational man paradigm by experimental
evidence is not new. As early as 1955 Simon asserted, "Recent
developments in economics . . . have raised great doubts as to
whether this schematized model of economic man provides a suitable foundation on which to erect a theory—whether it be a theory
of how firms *do* behave or of how they 'should' rationally behave."
Since then, a great deal of additional experimental evidence has
been accumulated, mainly by psychologists. Of particular interest
is the enormous literature initiated by Daniel Kahneman, Amos
Tversky, and their collaborators. We now have a fascinating com-
pilation of experimental data demonstrating the circumstances under which rationality breaks down and other patterns of behavior
emerge.

I will briefly dwell on a few examples that seem to me to be
especially strong in the sense that they not only demonstrate a
deviation from the rational man paradigm, but they also offer clues
about where to look for systematic alternatives. The order of the
examples parallels that of the discussion in the previous section.

Framing Effects

A rich body of literature has demonstrated circumstances under
which the assumption that two logically equivalent alternatives are
treated equally, does not hold. A beautiful demonstration of the

framing effect is the following experiment taken from Tversky and Kahneman (1986):

Subjects were told that an outbreak of a disease will cause six hundred people to die in the United States. Two mutually exclusive programs, yielding the following results, were considered:

A. two hundred people will be saved.

B. With a probability of 1/3, six hundred people will be saved; with a probability of 2/3, none will be saved.

Another group of subjects were asked to choose between two programs, yielding the results:

C. four hundred people will die.

D. With a probability of 1/3 no one will die; with a probability of 2/3 all six hundred will die.

Although 72 percent of the subjects chose A from {A, B}, 78 percent chose D from {C, D}. This occurred in spite of the fact that any reasonable man would say that A and C are identical and B and D are identical! One explanation for this phenomenon is that the description of the choice between A and B in terms of gains prompted risk aversion, whereas the description in terms of losses prompted risk loving.

Framing effects pose the most problematic challenges to the rationality paradigm. Their existence leads to the conclusion that an alternative has to appear in the model with its verbal description. Doing so is a challenging task beyond our reach at the moment.

The Tendency to Simplify a Problem
The following experiment is taken from Tversky and Kahneman (1986). Consider the lotteries A and B. Both involve spinning a roulette wheel. The colors, the prizes, and their probabilities are specified below:

A	Color	white	red	green	yellow
	Probability (%)	90	6	1	3
	Prize ($)	0	45	30	−15
B	Color	white	red	green	yellow
	Probability (%)	90	7	1	2
	Prize ($)	0	45	−10	−15

Facing the choice between A and B, about 58 percent of the subjects preferred A.

Now consider the two lotteries C and D:

C	Color	white	red	green	blue	yellow
	Probability (%)	90	6	1	1	2
	Prize ($)	0	45	30	−15	−15
D	Color	white	red	green	blue	yellow
	Probability (%)	90	6	1	1	2
	Prize ($)	0	45	45	−10	−15

The lottery D dominates C, and all subjects indeed chose D. However, notice that lottery B is, in all relevant respects, identical to lottery D (red and green in D are combined in B), and that A is the same as C (blue and yellow are combined in A).

What happened? As stated, decision makers try to simplify problems. "Similarity" relations are one of the basic tools they use for this purpose. When comparing A and B, many decision makers went through the following steps:

1. 6 and 7 percent, and likewise 2 and 3 percent, are similar;

2. The data about the probabilities and prizes for the colors white, red, and yellow is more or less the same for A and B, and

3. "Cancel" those components and you are left with comparing a gain of $30 with a loss of $10. This comparison, favoring A, is the decisive factor in determining that the lottery A is preferred to B.

By the way, when I conducted this experiment in class, there were (good!) students who preferred C over D after they preferred A over B. When asked to justify this "strange" choice, they pointed out that C is equivalent to A and D is equivalent to B and referred to their previous choice of A! These students demonstrated another common procedural element of decision making: The choice in one problem is made in relation to decisions made previously in response to other problems.

The Search for Reasons

In the next example (following Huber, Payne, and Puto [1982]), (x, y) represents a holiday package that contains x days in Paris and y days in London, all offered for the same price. All subjects agree that a day in London and a day in Paris are desirable goods. Denote, $A = (7, 4)$, $B = (4, 7)$, $C = (6, 3)$ and $D = (3, 6)$. Some of the subjects were requested to choose between the three packages A, B, and C; others had to choose between A, B, and D. The subjects exhibited a clear tendency to choose A out of the set $\{A, B, C\}$ and to choose B out of the set $\{A, B, D\}$. Obviously, this behavior is not consistent with the behavior of a "rational man." Given the universal preference of A over C and of B over D, the preferred element out of $\{A, B\}$ should be chosen from both $\{A, B, C\}$ and $\{A, B, D\}$.

Once again, the beauty of this example is not its contradiction of the rational man paradigm but its demonstration of a procedural element that often appears in decision making. Decision makers look for reasons to prefer A over B. Sometimes, those reasons relate to the decision problem itself. In the current example, "dominating another alternative" is a reason to prefer one alternative over the other. Reasons that involve relationships to other alternatives may therefore conflict with the rational man paradigm.

Another related, striking experiment was conducted by Tversky and Shafir (1992). A subject was shown a list of twelve cards. Each card described one prize. Then the subject was given two cards and asked whether he wanted to pay a certain fee for getting a third card from the deck. If he did not pay the fee, he had to choose one of the two prizes appearing on the cards in his hand. If he chose to pay the fee, he would have three cards, the two he had originally been dealt and the third he would now draw; he would then have to choose one among the three prizes.

The different configurations of prizes which appeared on the two cards given to the subjects were as follows:

1. Prizes A and B, where A dominates B;

2. Prizes A and C, where A and C are such that neither dominates the other.

A significantly lower percentage of subjects chose to pay the fee in face of (1) than in face of (2). Thus, once the decision maker has an "internal" reason (the domination of one over another alternative) to choose one of the alternatives, he is no longer interested in enriching the set of options. Many subjects, when confronted with conflict while making a choice, were ready to pay a fee for receipt of a reason that would help them to make the choice.

Remark One often hears criticism among economists of the experiments done by psychologists. Critics tend to focus blame on the fact that in the typical experimental design, subjects have no sufficient incentive to make the conduct of the experiment or its results relevant for economics—the rewards given were too small and the subjects were not trained to deal with the problems they faced. I disagree with this criticism for the following reasons:

• The experiments, I feel, simply confirmed solid intuitions originating from our own thought experiments.

• Many of the real-life problems we face entail small rewards and many of our daily decisions are made in the context of nonrecurring situations.

• When considering human behavior regarding "major" decisions, we observe severe conflicts with rationality as well. To illustrate,

Benartzi and Thaler (1995) discuss a survey regarding the choices made by university professors on the allocation of their investments in stocks and bonds within the TIAA-CREF pension fund. Although this decision is among the more important annual financial decisions made in the life of an American professor, the authors observe that the majority of investors divide their money between the two options in a manner almost impossible to rationalize as optimal in any form.

To summarize this section, we have reviewed several experiments that demonstrate motives for choice that are inconsistent with the rational man paradigm. The number of experiments undertaken, the clarity of the motives elicited, and their confirmation by our own "thought experiments" do not allow us to dismiss these experiments as curiosities.

1.5 Comments

Procedural and Substantive Rationality

The observation that behavior is not rational does not imply that it is chaotic. As already stated, the experiments discussed in the previous section hint at alternative elements of decision-making procedures that may establish the foundations for new economic models. Simon distinguishes between *substantive rationality* and *procedural rationality:* on one hand, substantive rationality refers to behavior that "is appropriate to the achievement of given goals within the limits imposed by given conditions and constraints"; on the other hand, "behavior is procedurally rational when it is the outcome of appropriate deliberation." That is, procedurally rational behavior is the outcome of some strategy of reasoning, whereas irrational behavior is an outcome of impulsive responses without adequate intervention of thought. In this book, we will drop the assumption of substantive rationality but retain that of procedural rationality.

Mistakes vs. Bounded Rationality

Some have claimed that the phenomena demonstrated in the above experiments are uninteresting inasmuch as they express "mistakes" that disappear once the subjects learn of their existence. They contend that economists are not interested in traders who believe that $1 + 1 = 3$; similarly, they should not be interested in agents who are subject to framing affects.

I beg to differ. Labeling behavior as "mistakes" does make the behavior uninteresting. If there are many traders in a market who calculate $1 + 1 = 3$, then their "mistake" may be economically relevant. The fact that behavior may be changed after the subjects have been informed of their "mistakes" is of interest, but so is behavior absent the revelation of mistakes because, in real life, explicit "mistake-identifiers" rarely exist.

Rationalizing on a Higher Level

As economists raised on the rational man paradigm, our natural response to the idea of describing a decision maker by starting from a decision procedure is akin to asking the question, "Where does the procedure come from?" One method of rationalizing the use of decision procedures inconsistent with the rational man paradigm is by expanding the context to that of a "richer" decision problem in which additional considerations (such as the cost of deliberation) are taken into account. Under such conditions, one may try to argue that what seems to be irrational is actually rational. In regard to the satisficing procedure (P-2), for example, such a question was asked and answered by Simon himself. Simon proposed a search model with costs in order to derive the use of the procedure and to provide an explanation for the determination of the aspiration value.

This is an interesting research program, but I do not see why we *must* follow it. Alternatively, we may treat the level of aspiration simply as one parameter of the decision maker's problem (similar to the coefficient in a Cobb-Douglas utility function in standard consumer theory), a parameter that is not selected by the decision maker but is given among his exogenous characteristics. We should probably view rationality as a property of behavior *within* the model. The fact that having an aspiration level is justifiable as rational behavior in one model does not mean that we can consider that behavior as rational within any other model.

1.6 Bibliographic Notes

The pioneering works on bounded rationality are those of Herbert Simon. See, for example, Simon (1955, 1956, 1972, and 1976). (About the first two papers Simon wrote: "If I were asked to select just two of my publications in economics for transmission to another galaxy where intelligent life had just been discovered, these are the two I would choose.") All four papers are reprinted in Simon (1982).

For the foundation of choice theory see, for example, Kreps (1988).

The material on experimental decision theory has been surveyed recently in Camerer (1994) and Shafir and Tversky (1995). For a more detailed discussion of the framing effect see Tversky and Kahneman (1986). The experiments on reason-based choice are summarized in Shafir, Simonson, and Tversky (1993) and Tversky and Shafir (1992). See also Simonson (1989) and Huber, Payne, and Puto (1982). The tendency to simplify complicated problems to more manageable ones is discussed in Payne, Battman, and Johnson (1988).

1.7 Projects

1. *Reading* Shafir, Diamond, and Tversky (1997) reports on a "framing effect" in the context of economic decisions in times of inflation. Read the paper and suggest another context in which a similar "framing effect" may influence economic behavior.

2. *Reading* Read Benartzi and Thaler (1995) on the decision of real investors to allocate their investments between stocks and bonds. Consider the following "experiment." Subjects are split into two groups. At each of the two periods of the experiment, each subject gets a fixed income that he must invest immediately in stocks and bonds. At the end of the first period, an investor has access to information about that period's yields. A subject cashes his investments at the end of the second period.

At every period, a member of the first group is asked to allocate only the income he receives that period, whereas a member of the second group is asked to reallocate his *entire* balance at that point.

Guess the two typical responses. Can such an experiment establish that investors' behaviors are not compatible with rationality?

3. *Innovative* Choose one of the axiomatizations of decision making under uncertainly (exclude the original expected utility axiomatization) and examine the axiom from a procedural point of view.

2   Modeling Procedural Decision Making

2.1 Motivation

In the previous chapter, I argued that experimental evidence from the psychological literature demonstrates the existence of common procedural elements that are quite distinct from those involved in the rational man's decision-making mechanism. In this chapter, we turn to a discussion of attempts to model formally some of these elements.

Note that when we model procedural aspects of decision making, we are not necessarily aiming at the construction of models of choice that are incompatible with rationality. Our research program is to model formally procedures of choice that exhibit a certain procedural element, and then to investigate whether or not such procedures are compatible with rationality. If they are, we will try to identify restrictions on the space of preferences that are compatible with those procedures.

We now return to a motive we mentioned in Chapter 1: Decision makers attempt to simplify decision problems. For simplicity, let us focus on choice problems that contain two alternatives, each described as a vector. One way to simplify such a problem is to apply similarity notions in order to "cancel" the components of the two alternatives that are alike, and thereby to reduce the number of elements involved in the descriptions of the two alternatives. This makes the comparison less cumbersome.

To illustrate, let us look at results of an experiment, reported in Kahneman and Tversky (1982), that is similar to that of the Allais paradox. The objects of choice in the experiment are simple lotteries. A *simple lottery* (x,p) is a random variable that yields $\$x$ with probability p and $\$0$ with probability $1 - p$. Thus, each object of choice can be thought of as a vector of length 2.

In the experiment, some subjects were asked to choose between:

$L_3 = (4000, 0.2)$ and $L_4 = (3000, 0.25)$.

Most subjects chose L_3. Another group of subjects was asked to choose between:

$L_1 = (4000, 0.8)$ and $L_2 = (3000, 1.0)$.

The vast majority of subjects chose L_2.

The choices L_2 from $\{L_1, L_2\}$ and L_3 from $\{L_3, L_4\}$ do not violate rationality. However, they do violate the von Neumann-Morgenstern independence axiom. To see this, notice that the lotteries L_3 and L_4 can be presented as compound lotteries of L_1, L_2, and the degenerate lottery $[0]$, which yields the certain prize 0:

$L_3 = 0.25L_1 + 0.75[0]$ and $L_4 = 0.25L_2 + 0.75[0]$.

Therefore, the independence axiom requires that the choice between L_3 and L_4 be made according to the choice between L_1 and L_2, in striking contrast to the experimental results.

The reasoning that probably guided many of the subjects was the following: When comparing L_3 to L_4, a decision maker faces an internal conflict due to the higher prize in L_3 versus the higher probability of getting a positive prize in L_4. He tries to simplify the choice problem so that one of the alternatives will be patently better. With this aim, he checks the similarities of the probabilities and the prizes that appear in the two lotteries. He considers the probability numbers 0.25 and 0.2 to be similar, in contrast to the prizes $\$4000$ and $\$3000$, which are not. These similarity comparisons lead him to "simplify" the problem by "canceling" the probabilities and making the choice between L_3 and L_4, based on the obvious choice between \$4000 and \$3000. On the other hand, when comparing L_1 and L_2, the decision maker cannot simplify the problem on the basis of the cancellation of similar components since neither the probabilities nor the prizes are perceived to be similar. He then invokes another principle, presumably risk aversion, to arrive at the superiority of L_2.

Note that the attractiveness of the vNM independence axiom is also related to its interpretation as an expression of a similar procedural element. When the lotteries L_3 and L_4 are represented explicitly in the form of the reduced lotteries $0.25L_1 + 0.75[0]$ and $0.25L_2 + 0.75[0]$, respectively, decision makers tend to simplify the comparison between L_3 and L_4 by "canceling" the possibility that the lotteries will yield the prize $[0]$, then basing their choice on a comparison between L_1 and L_2, thus choosing L_4.

Hence, whether the lotteries are presented as simple or compound, it seems that a major step in the deliberation is the "cancellation of similar factors" and the consequent reduction of the original complex choice to a simpler one. Activating this principle when comparing L_3 and L_4 as simple lotteries leads to the choice of L_3; activating it when the lotteries are presented as compound lotteries leads to the choice of L_4. The way in which the principle of reducing the complexity of a choice is applied, therefore, depends on how the decision problem is framed. To avoid framing effects in our analysis, we will retain the format of each alternative as fixed. Consequently, all objects of choice will be simple lotteries presented as vectors of the type (x, p).

In the next three sections we will formulate and analyze a procedure for choosing between pairs of such lotteries that makes explicit use of similarity relations. The presentation consists of the following stages. First we will describe a scheme of choice procedures between pairs of lotteries. Then we will ask two questions:

1. Does such a procedure necessarily conflict with the rational man paradigm?

2. If not, what preference relations are consistent with the procedure?

But first we will detour to the world of similarity relations in order to equip ourselves with the necessary tools.

2.2 Preparing the Tools: Similarity Relations

In this chapter, a *similarity relation* is taken to be a binary relation $\sim$ on the set $I = [0, 1]$ that satisfies the following properties:

(S-1) *Reflexivity* For all $a \in I$, $a \sim a$.

(S-2) *Symmetry* For all $a, b \in I$, if $a \sim b$, then $b \sim a$.

(S-3) *Continuity* The graph of the relation $\sim$ is closed in $I \times I$.

(S-4) *Betweenness* If $a \leq b \leq c \leq d$ and $a \sim d$, then $b \sim c$.

(S-5) *Nondegeneracy* $0 \nsim 1$, and for all $0 < a < 1$, there are b and c so that $b < a < c$ and $a \sim b$ and $a \sim c$. For $a = 1$, there is $b < a$ so that $a \sim b$. (For reasons which will soon become clear, no such requirement is made for $a = 0$.)

(S-6) *Responsiveness* Denote by a^* and a_* the largest and the smallest elements in the set that are similar to a. Then a^* and a_* are strictly increasing functions (in a) at any point at which they obtain a value different from 0 or 1.

Although these axioms restrict the notion of similarity quite significantly, I find them particularly suitable when the similarity stands for a relation of the kind "approximately the same." This does not deny that there are contexts in which the notion of similarity clearly does not satisfy the above axioms. For example, we say that "Luxembourg is similar to Belgium," but we do not say that "Belgium is similar to Luxembourg" (see Tversky [1977]). In this example, we say that "a is similar to b" in the sense that b is a "representative" of the class of elements to which both a and b belong; this use of the term does not satisfy the symmetry condition.

A leading example of a family of relations that satisfies all these assumptions is the one consisting of the λ-ratio similarity relations (with $\lambda > 1$) defined by $a \sim b$ if $1/\lambda \leq a/b \leq \lambda$. More generally, for any number $\lambda > 1$ and for every strictly increasing continuous function, H, on the unit interval, the relation $a \sim b$ if $1/\lambda \leq H(a)/H(b) \leq \lambda$ is a similarity relation. In fact, we can represent any similarity relation in this way. We say that the pair (H, λ) *represents* the similarity relation $\sim$ if, for all $a,b \in I$, $a \sim b$ if $1/\lambda \leq H(a)/H(b) \leq \lambda$. One can show (see Project 6) that for every $\lambda > 1$ there is a strictly increasing continuous function H with values in $[0, 1]$, so that the pair (H, λ) represents the similarity $\sim$. If 0 is not similar to any positive number, we can find a representation of the similarity relation with a function H so that $H(0) = 0$. This proposition is analogous to propositions in utility theory that show the existence of a certain functional form of a utility representation.

Note that no equivalence relation is a similarity relation under this definition. Consider, for example, the relation according to which any two elements in I relate if, in their decimal presentation, they have identical first digits. This binary relation is an equivalence relation that fails to comply with the continuity assumption, the monotonicity assumption (because $(.13)_* = (.14)_*$, for example), and the nondegeneracy condition (there is no $x < 0.4$ that relates to 0.4).

2.3 A Procedure of Choice between Vectors

In this section we analyze a family of decision procedures applied to decision problems where the choice is made from a set of pairs of lotteries in $\mathbf{A} = X \times P = [0, 1] \times [0, 1]$, where $(x, p) \in \mathbf{A}$ stands for a simple lottery that awards the prizes $x with probability p and $0 with the residual probability $1 - p$.

(P-*) The primitives of the procedure are two similarity relations, $\sim_x$ and $\sim_p$, that relate to the objects in X and P, respectively. (Thus, we do not require that the same similarity relation be relevant to both dimensions.) When choosing between the two lotteries $L_1 = (x_1, p_1)$ and $L_2 = (x_2, p_2)$:

Step 1 (Check domination):

If both $x_i > x_j$ and $p_i > p_j$, then choose L_i;

If Step 1 is not decisive, move to Step 2, in which the similarity relations are invoked. This step is the heart of our procedure in that it captures the intuitions gained from the psychological experiments.

Step 2 (Check similarities):

If $p_i \sim_p p_j$ and not $x_i \sim_x x_j$, and $x_i > x_j$, then choose L_i.

If $x_i \sim_x x_j$ and not $p_i \sim_p p_j$, and $p_i > p_j$, then choose L_i.

If Step 2 is also not decisive, then move to Step 3, which is not specified.

We move on to study the compatibility of following (P-*) with the rational man procedure. Note that all vectors of the type $(x, 0)$ or $(0, p)$ are identical lotteries that yield the prize 0 with certainty. Therefore, in the following, preferences on $X \times P$ are assumed to have an indifference curve that coincides with the axis. The following definition defines the compatibility of a preference relation with (P-*). We say that a preference relation $\succsim$ is *(\sim_x, \sim_p)$ consistent if for any pair of lotteries L_i and L_j, if L_i is chosen in one of the first two steps of the procedure, then $L_i > L_j$. In other words, any of the following three conditions implies that $L_i > L_j$:

1. Both $x_i > x_j$ and $p_i > p_j$

2. $p_i \sim_p p_j$ and not $x_i \sim_x x_j$, and also $x_i > x_j$

3. $x_i \sim_x x_j$ and not $p_i \sim_p p_j$, and also $p_i > p_j$.

Example Let $\succsim$ be a preference represented by the utility function px^α. Then $\succsim$ is consistent with (P-∗) where $\sim_x$ and $\sim_p$ are the λ and λ^α ratio similarities. For example, condition (2) implies $L_i > L_j$ because if $p_i \sim_p p_j$, not $x_i \sim_x x_j$, and $x_i > x_j$, then $p_i x_i^\alpha > p_i(\lambda x_j)^\alpha = (p_i\lambda^\alpha)x_j^\alpha \geq p_j x_j^\alpha$.

2.4 Analysis

We now turn to an analysis of the decision procedures defined in the previous section. Our general program, applied to the current setting, includes the following questions:

1. Given a pair of similarity relations, are the decisions implied by Steps 1 and 2 of (P-∗) consistent with the optimization of any preference relation?

2. How does (P-∗) restrict the set of preferences that are consistent with the procedure?

First, note the following simple observation. Unless we assume that there is no x so that $0 \sim_x x$ and no p so that $0 \sim_p p$, there is no preference that is ∗($\sim_x$, $\sim_p$) consistent. Assume, for example, that $x \sim_x 0$ and $x \neq 0$. Then, if there is a preference that is ∗($\sim_x$, $\sim_p$) consistent, the degenerate lottery $(0, 1)$ has to be preferred to $(x, 1_* - \varepsilon)$ for some $\varepsilon > 0$ (by Step 2) and $(x, 1_* - \varepsilon)$ has to be preferred to $(0, 0)$ (by Step 1). Thus $(0, 0)$ cannot be indifferent to $(0, 1)$, as we assumed.

The next proposition provides an answer to the first question. For any pair of similarity relations there are preferences that do not contradict the execution of the first two steps of (P-∗) with those two similarity relations. Thus, (P-∗) does not necessarily conflict with the rational man paradigm.

Proposition 2.1 Let $\sim_x$ and $\sim_p$ be similarity relations satisfying that there is no $x \neq 0$ or $p \neq 0$ with $0 \sim_x x$ or $0 \sim_p p$. Then, there are functions $u: X \to R^+$ and $g: P \to R^+$, so that $g(p)u(x)$ represents a preference on $X \times P$ that is $*(\sim_x, \sim_p)$ consistent.

Proof Let $\lambda > 1$. From the previous section, there exist non-negative strictly increasing continuous functions, u and g, with $u(0) = g(0) = 0$, so that (u, λ) and (g, λ) represent the similarities $\sim_x$ and $\sim_p$, respectively.

The function $g(p)u(x)$ assigns the utility 0 to all lotteries on the axes. We will show that $g(p)u(x)$ induces a preference that is $*(\sim_x, \sim_p)$ consistent. Assume that both $x_i > x_j$ and $p_i > p_j$; then $g(p_i)u(x_i) > g(p_j)u(x_j)$, thus $L_i > L_j$. Assume that $p_i \sim_p p_j$, not $x_i \sim_x x_j$, and $x_i > x_j$; then $u(x_i) > \lambda u(x_j)$, $g(p_i) \geq (1/\lambda)g(p_j)$, and hence $g(p_i)u(x_i) > g(p_j)u(x_j)$; so that, $L_i > L_j$. □

Note that this proof implies that there are not only preferences consistent with the first two steps of the procedure but also preferences consistent with the first two steps that have an *additive* utility representation.

We now approach the second question. Proposition 2.3 shows that few preferences are consistent with (P-*). For any pair of similarities $\sim_x$ and $\sim_p$, the preference relation built in the last proposition is "the almost unique" preference that is $*(\sim_x, \sim_p)$ consistent. Thus the assumption that a decision maker uses a (P-*) procedure with a pair of similarity relations narrows down the consistent preferences to almost a unique preference whose maximization explains the decision maker's behavior.

The following proposition provides the key argument:

Proposition 2.2 Consider a preference $\gtrsim$ on $X \times P$ that is $*(\sim_x, \sim_p)$ consistent. For any (x, p) with $x^* < 1$ and $p^* < 1$, all lotteries that dominate (x^*, p_*) (or (x_*, p^*)) are preferred to (x, p), and all lotteries that are dominated by (x^*, p_*) (or (x_*, p^*)) are inferior to (x, p). (If the preference is continuous, then it follows that the preference assigns indifference between (x, p) and (x^*, p_*).)

Proof By Step 2 of the procedure, $(x, p) < (x^* + \varepsilon, p_*)$ for all $\varepsilon > 0$. Any lottery that dominates (x^*, p_*) must also dominate some lottery $(x^* + \varepsilon, p_*)$ for ε small enough, thus is preferred to (x, p). Similarly, $(x, p) > (x^*, p_* - \varepsilon)$ for all $\varepsilon > 0$; thus, we also obtain that (x, p) is preferred to any lottery that is dominated by (x^*, p_*). $\square$

We will now show that for any two preferences $\succeq$ and $\succeq'$, which are $*(\sim_x, \sim_p)$ consistent, and for every pair of lotteries L_1 and L_2 so that $L_1 > L_2$, there must be a lottery L_2' "close" to L_2 so that $L_1 >' L_2'$. Thus, although there may be many preference relations consistent with the first two stages of (P-*), they are all "close." The two first steps of the procedure "almost" determine a unique preference where closeness is evaluated in terms of the similarity relations.

Proposition 2.3 If $\succeq$ and $\succeq'$ are both consistent with the pair of similarities $(\sim_x, \sim_p)$, then for any (x_1, p_1) and (x_2, p_2) satisfying $(x_1, p_1) > (x_2, p_2)$, there are $x_2' \sim_x x_2$ and $p_2' \sim_p p_2$ such that $(x_1, p_1) >' (x_2', p_2')$.

Proof Consider the figure 2.1.

By Proposition 2.2, any preference that is $*(\sim_x, \sim_p)$ consistent must satisfy the condition that all points in area A are preferred to $L_1 = (x, p)$ and L_1 is preferred to any point in area B. (Actually, if the preference is continuous, then its indifference curve, passing through L_1, includes the lotteries indicated by dots.) Thus, if both $\succeq$ and $\succeq'$ are $*(\sim_x, \sim_p)$ consistent, and $L_1 > L_2$ and not $L_1 >' L_2$, then L_2 must be outside areas A and B. But then, there is a lottery L_2' "close to L_2" in the sense that both the x and the p components of L_2 and L_2' are $\sim_x$ and $\sim_p$ similar, so that $L_1 >' L_2'$. $\square$

Discussion This proposition shows, in my opinion, that Steps 1 and 2 "overdetermine" the preference. Even before specifying the content of Step 3, we arrive at an almost unique preference that is

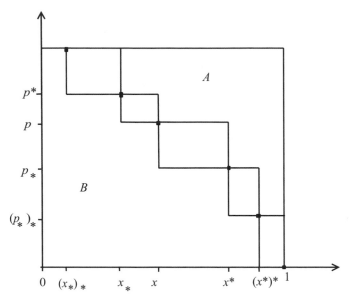

Figure 2.1

consistent with the choices determined by applying only Steps 1 and 2. The overdetermination result casts doubts as to whether decision makers who use such a procedure can be described as optimizers of preferences.

However, one can interpret the analysis of this section as a derivation of separable preference relations. Any preference consistent with (P-∗) must be close to a preference relation represented by a utility function of the type $g(p)u(x)$. The key to this separability result is that the similarities are assumed to be "global" in the sense that when examining the two lotteries (x_1, p_1) and (x_2, p_2), the determination of whether x_1 is similar to x_2 is done independently of the values of the probabilities p_1 and p_2.

2.5 Case-Based Theory

We now turn to a short discussion of a formalization of "case-based theory," an interesting model of choice that captures procedural elements of decision making that are quite different from the ingredients of the rational man procedure.

Case-based theory is designed to describe a decision maker who bases decisions on the consequences derived from past actions taken in relevant, similar cases. Take, for instance, the American decision whether to send troops to Bosnia in late 1995. When considering this problem, decision makers had in mind several previous events during which American troops were sent on interventionary missions on foreign soil (Vietnam, Lebanon and the Persian Gulf). Those instances were offered as relevant precedents for the proposed action. The decision whether to interfere in Bosnia was taken, to a large extent, on the basis of evaluations of the past events and the assessment of the similarity of those cases to the Bosnian case.

In the model, a decision maker has to choose among members of a fixed set A. Let $\mathbf{P}$ be a set whose elements are called *problems*. An element in $\mathbf{P}$ is a description of the circumstances under which an alternative from the set A has to be chosen. The problems in $\mathbf{P}$ are related in the sense that the experience of one problem is conceived by the decision maker as relevant for another problem. Let $\mathbf{C}$ be a set of consequences; for simplicity, we take $\mathbf{C} = \mathbf{R}$, the set of real numbers. Taking an action in a problem deterministically yields a consequence, but the connection between the action and the consequence is unknown to the decision maker unless he has already experienced it.

An instance of experience, a *case*, is a triple (p, a, u) interpreted as an event in which, at the problem p, the action a was taken and yielded the consequence u. A *memory*, M, is a finite set of cases. Note that the notion of memory here abstracts from the temporal order of the experienced cases. An instance of decision is a pair (p^*, M): the decision maker has to choose an element from the set A, at the problem $p^* \in \mathbf{P}$, given the memory M. We assume that for each memory, all problems are distinct, that is, for any (p, a, u) and

(p', a', u') in M, $p \neq p'$ (compare with Project 8). Finally, a *choice function* assigns to each problem p^* and memory M, an action in A.

The procedure described by Gilboa and Schmeidler (1995) is as follows. The primitive of the procedure is a measure of closeness between problems, $s(p, p')$. Each $s(p, p')$ is a non-negative number with the interpretation that the higher the $s(p, p')$, more similar is p' to p. Given a problem p^* and a memory M, each action $a \in A$ is evaluated by the number $v(a, p^*, M) = \Sigma_{(p,a,u) \in M} s(p^*, p)u$. In case action a was not examined in the memory M, $v(a, p^*, M)$ is taken to be 0. The decision maker chooses an action $a \in A$ that maximizes $v(a, p^*, M)$ (given some tie-breaking rule).

Recall that in this model, the set A is fixed and a decision maker bases his decision regarding one problem on past experiences with other problems. The model allows phrasing of consistency conditions that link different memories rather than different choice sets as in the rational choice theory.

Gilboa and Schmeidler offer several axiomatizations of the above procedure. The basic axiomatization is based on the following (strong) assumption: A decision maker facing the problem p^* and having the memory M, "transforms" each action a into a vector $z(a, M) \in Z = \mathbf{R}^P$ (the set of functions that assign a real number to each problem in P, the set of problems experienced in M). He does so as follows: If $(p, a, u) \in M$, (that is, if the action a was taken when confronting the problem p), then $z(a, M)(p) = u$; otherwise (that is, if the action a was not attempted at the problem p), we take $z(a, M)(p) = 0$. It is assumed that the decision maker has in mind a preference relation $\succsim_{p^*}$ defined on the set Z so that at the problem p^*, having the memory M, he chooses an action a^* satisfying $z(a^*, M) \succsim_{p^*} z(a, M)$ for all $a \in A$.

Given this assumption, we are left with the need to axiomatize the preference relation on Z. We have to show that there are coefficients, $\{s(p, p^*)\}_{p,p^* \in P}$, so that this preference relation has a utility representation of the type $\Sigma_{p \in P} s(p, p^*) z_p$. This requires additional assumptions that induce a linearity structure. This can be done in a variety of ways: for example, by requiring that $\succsim$ satisfies monotonicity, continuity, and, most important, a property called separability: for any $x, y, w, z \in Z$, if $x \succsim y$ and $w \succsim z$, then $x + w \succsim y + z$ (with strict preference in case $w \succ z$).

This axiomatization is quite problematic. A preference is defined on the large set Z. This implies that the decision maker is required to compare vectors that cannot be realized in any memory (the decision maker will never have two different cases, such as (p, a, u) and (p, a', u') in his memory; yet the preference on the set $\mathbf{R}^P$ exhibits comparisons between vectors z and z' with both $z_p \neq 0$ and $z'_p \neq 0$). The separability axiom is quite arbitrary. As to the interpretation of $s(p, p^*)$ as a "degree of similarity," because the axiomatization treats the behavior at any two problems completely separately, there are no restrictions on the similarity function. It might be, for example, that $s(p^*, p^{**}) = 1$, whereas $s(p^{**}, p^*) = 0$ making the interpretation of the numbers $\{s(p, p')\}$ as a similarity measure questionable.

2.6 Bibliographic Notes

Sections 1–4 are based on Rubinstein (1988). For previous related work, see Luce (1956) and Ng (1977). The role of similarities in human reasoning was emphasized by Amos Tversky in a series of papers. In particular, see Tversky (1969) and Tversky (1977).

Section 5 is based on Gilboa and Schmeidler (1995, 1997). See also Matsui (1994).

2.7 Projects

1. *Innovative* Tversky (1977) shows that in some contexts similarity relations may be asymmetric relations. Suggest a context in which such asymmetry is relevant to choice.

2. *Reading* Why are two objects perceived to be similar? One response is that an object a is similar to an object b when the number of properties (unary relations)

that are satisfied by both a and b is "large enough." However, Watanabe (1969) argues against this concept through the "Ugly Duckling Theorem" (Section 7.6): If the set of unary predicates is closed under Boolean operations, then the number of predicates that satisfy any possible object is constant. Prove the theorem and explain in what sense it is a blow to this approach.

3. *Innovative* Propose several examples of relations you would call "similarity relations" in the natural language and ascertain whether they comply with the definition of similarity relations given in this chapter.

4. *Reading* Read Luce (1956) and explain the connection between the formalization of similarity relations and Luce's concept of semi-order.

5. *Exercise* Fill in the gaps in the proof of the proposition stating that if $\sim$ is a similarity relation, then for every $\lambda > 1$ there is a strictly increasing continuous function H that takes values in the interval $[0, 1]$ so that (H, λ) represents $\sim$.
Hint Define, by induction, a sequence (x^n) such that $x^0 = 1$ and $x^n + 1 = (x^n)_*$. By (S-3), x^{n+1} is well defined. By (S-5), $x^n \to 0$. Define $H(1) = 1$. Define $H: [x^1, x^0] \to \mathbf{R}$ as any strictly increasing continuous function satisfying $H(x^0) = 1$ and $H(x^1) = 1/\lambda$. For $x \in [x^{n+1}, x^n]$, define $H(x) = H(x^*)/\lambda$. By (S-6), the function H is strictly increasing. If 0 is not similar to any x, define $H(0) = 0$ (otherwise there is an n such that $x^n = 0$). Verify that (H, λ) represents $\sim$.

6. *Exercise* Assume that $\gtrsim$ is represented by the utility function $g(p)u(x)$, where g and u are positive, strictly increasing continuous functions. Show that if $\gtrsim$ is $*(\sim_x, \sim_p)$ consistent, then there is a $\lambda > 1$ such that

$x_1 \sim_x x_2$ iff $1/\lambda < u(x_2)/u(x_1) < \lambda$ and

$p_1 \sim_p p_2$ iff $1/\lambda < g(p_2)/g(p_1) < \lambda$.

Conclude that the vNM expected utility theory together with (P-*) requires that $\sim_p$ be a λ-ratio similarity relation. (Analogously, the dual expected utility theory, which has a utility representation with the functional form $g(p)x$, requires that $\sim_x$ be a λ-ratio similarity relation.)

7. *Reading* Read Azipurua, Ichiishi, Nieto, and Uriarte (1993), who extend the results of this chapter to the case where the determination of whether x_1 is similar to x_2 is *not* done independently of the relevant probabilities p_1 and p_2.

8. *Innovative* Consider the following variant of case-based theory where all problems are identical (therefore, we can omit the symbol $\mathbf{P}$ from the model). A memory M is now a set of pairs (a, u) with the interpretation that action a was taken and yielded payoff u. Retain the assumption that any action determines one consequence: In a memory M, there are no two cases where $(a, u) \neq (a, u')$. A choice function here assigns an element in A to each memory. Note that in this context, case-based theory is equivalent to the satisficing procedure. Thus, a decision maker chooses new alternatives until he finds an action with a strictly positive consequence.

Check whether the following properties of a choice function c are satisfied by the above procedure and whether the properties provide a proper axiomatization:

Neutrality (invariance to the names of the actions) If $(c(M), u)$ is a case in M, then for any σ, a permutation of A, $c(\sigma(M)) = \sigma(c(M))$ where $\sigma(M)$ is the memory obtained from M by replacing (a, u) with $(\sigma(a), u)$.

Monotonicity Assume that M contains the case $(c(M), u)$. Let M' be a memory identical to M except that the case $(c(M), u)$ is replaced with $(c(M), u')$, where $u' > u$. Then $c(M) = c(M')$.

Independence of Irrelevant Alternatives If $(c(M), u)$ is a case in M, then $c(M') = c(M)$ for any $M' \subseteq M$ that contains the case $(c(M), u)$.

9. *Innovative* For the model described in the previous project, construct plausible alternative decision procedures and study their properties. (An idea for an alternative procedure: A function $\varepsilon(a, a')$ measures "distance" between pairs of *actions a* and a'. Given a memory M, the decision maker chooses the action a^* if the case (a^*, u^*) is in M and for any other action a', there is a case (a'', u'') in M with $u^* \geq u'' + \varepsilon(a', a'')$. Otherwise, he chooses an action that was not experienced.)

3

Modeling Knowledge

3.1 Knowledge and Bounded Rationality

In the previous chapters, we referred to the rational man as a decision maker who holds preferences and chooses the best alternative from the set of feasible alternatives. But when economists use the term "rationality," they require not only that a chosen action be the best possible given the decision maker's knowledge, but also that the knowledge employed be derived from coherent inferences. Consider, for example, a decision maker who thinks that if it is not raining, his window is dry, and that if it is raining, he might or might not see drops of water on his window. Rationality implies that if he sees drops of water on his window, he concludes that it is raining. In contrast, models of bounded rationality are intended to allow us to talk about agents who systematically do not make correct inferences.

We will open this chapter by a short presentation of the model of knowledge used in economics. This model will also serve as the cornerstone for attempts to model systematic deviations from the making of perfect inferences.

3.2 Information Structure

The following is the standard model of knowledge, associated with Hintikka. An *information structure* is a pair (Ω, P) whose first component, Ω, is a set of *states*. Usually, we take a state to be a "full description of the world" or, at least, the relevant (for decision making) facts about the world. The states are taken to be mutually exclusive. The second component is a function P that assigns to each state ω a non-empty subset of states, $P(\omega)$. The major interpretation of P is that at the state ω, the inference maker excludes all the states outside $P(\omega)$, and does not exclude any states in $P(\omega)$. The assumption that $P(\omega) \neq \varnothing$ means that the decision maker cannot be so "wrong" as to exclude all possible states as being feasible.

The model is very simple and, as often happens with overly abstract models, the overabstraction is a cause of vagueness in its interpretation. The question "What is a state?" is at the center of the controversy. What, precisely, do we include in the "full description of the world"? There are two major issues involved:

1. Clearly, we wish a state to include a description of the resolution of all uncertainties that influence the decision maker's interests. However, within that "full description" we may also include the evidence received by the decision maker and the inferences he does or does not make. Thus, Ω may include a state "no rain" as well as "rain1," a state in which there is rain but the decision maker does not observe any signal alluding to this fact; "rain2," a state in which he observes drops on the window and concludes that it is raining; and state "rain3," in which he sees the drops but does not conclude that it is raining.

2. Does a full description of a state pertaining to a decision problem also specify the action to be taken by the decision maker? If we were to include the action within the description of a state, the assumption would be, at least superficially, in disharmony with the notion of free will. Nonetheless, many recent papers that derive game-theoretic solution concepts from models of knowledge take a state to be "an ideal, full description of the world including the choice of the decision maker." Note that if we adopt this understanding, we have to talk about the rationality of a decision maker

in reference to a specific state. It is possible that the decision maker is rational in one state and is not rational in another state.

The model does not specify the methods by which the decision maker makes the inferences by which he excludes certain states. More specifically, the content of the states reflects only the *outcome* of the decision maker's inference process. As such, the model has to be thought of as a reduced form derived from a more complete model, one that captures the decision maker's inference process.

We now turn to a discussion of the three properties of information structures usually associated with the term "rationality."

P-1 $\omega \in P(\omega)$.

P-1 expresses the condition that the decision maker never excludes the true state from the set of feasible states.

P-2   If $\omega' \in P(\omega)$, then $P(\omega') \subseteq P(\omega)$.

It is impossible for a decision maker who satisfies P-2 to hold the view that $\omega' \in P(\omega)$, despite there being a state z, so that $z \in P(\omega')$ and $z \notin P(\omega)$. Assume that $z \in P(\omega')$ and $z \notin P(\omega)$. Then, at, ω a rational decision maker could make the consideration: "The state z is excluded. Were the state ω', I would not exclude z. Thus, it must be that the state is not ω'." This inference contradicts the assumption that $\omega' \in P(\omega)$.

P-3   If $\omega' \in P(\omega)$, then $P(\omega') \supseteq P(\omega)$.

Consider the case that $\omega' \in P(\omega)$ and there is a state $z \in P(\omega)$ that is not in $P(\omega')$. Then, at ω, a rational decision maker can conclude, from the fact that he cannot exclude z, that the state is not ω', a state at which he would be able to exclude z, contradicting the assumption that $\omega' \in P(\omega)$.

Notice that if an information structure satisfies P-1 and P-3, it also satisfies P-2: If $\omega' \in P(\omega)$, then by P-3 $P(\omega') \supseteq P(\omega)$, by P-1 $\omega \in P(\omega)$, and thus $\omega \in P(\omega')$ which, again by P-3, implies that $P(\omega) \supseteq P(\omega')$.

Rationality regarding knowledge is defined by an information structure that satisfies the three properties P-1, 2, 3. Proposition 3.1 shows that the combination of these three properties is equivalent to the assumption that the information structure is *partitional*, namely, that there exists a partition of Ω (that is, a collection of mutually exclusive subsets of Ω that completely cover Ω) such that $P(\omega)$ is the set, within the partition, that includes ω.

Proposition 3.1 An information structure (Ω, P) is partitional if and only if it satisfies P-1, 2, 3.

Proof Clearly, a partitional information structure satisfies the three properties. On the other hand, if (Ω, P) satisfies P-1, 2, 3, define a relation R by $\omega \, R \, \omega'$ if $P(\omega) = P(\omega')$. The relation R is an equivalence relation and, therefore, induces a partition on Ω. Assume that $\omega \in X$ where X is a set in this partition. We have to show that $P(\omega) = X$. If $\omega' \in X$, then $P(\omega') = P(\omega)$, and because by P-1, $\omega' \in P(\omega')$, $\omega' \in P(\omega)$, and thus $P(\omega) \supseteq X$. If $\omega' \in P(\omega)$, then by P-2 and P-3, $P(\omega') = P(\omega)$ and thus $\omega' \in X$ so that $X \supseteq P(\omega)$. $\square$

We now move to inspect examples of information structures. Each example includes details about an inference method applicable in a specific context. Some of the examples demonstrate systematic imperfections in making inferences that reflect violations of P-1, P-2, or P-3.

Examples

In the first four examples, we take Ω to be the set of two digit-numbers, $\{00, 01, \ldots, 99\}$.

Example 1 The decision maker recognizes only the ones digit. Then for any $n \in \Omega$, $P(n) = \{n' \mid$ the ones digit of n' is identical to that of $n\}$. P is partitional and each cell contains ten states with the same ones digit.

Example 2 (Awareness) It often occurs that a decision maker is becoming aware of an event when it happens but does not notice the fact that the event does not happen when it does not happen. For example, assume that the decision maker at state ω perceives the ones digit and that he takes notice whenever the two digits in ω are identical; but, when the two digits are different, he does not pay attention to the "same digits" attribute. Thus, for example, $P(23) = \{?3 \mid ?$ is a digit$\}$, whereas $P(33) = \{33\}$. This information structure satisfies P-1 and P-2 but does not satisfy P-3: $33 \in P(23)$ but $23 \in P(23)$ and $23 \notin P(33)$. The decision maker, at 23, makes no inferences from the fact that he does not conclude that the state is 33.

Example 3 (Accuracy) The states 00 to 99 are read on a meter with a reading error of 1. That is, at state n, the decision maker can be sure only that the real state is nothing but $n - 1$, n, or $n + 1$. Thus, $P(n) = \{n - 1, n, n + 1\}$ for all n except 00 and 99, where $P(00) = \{00, 01\}$ and $P(99) = \{98, 99\}$. This information structure satisfies P-1 but not P-2 or P-3.

Example 4 (Systematic Mistakes) The decision maker makes a systematic mistake in observation: he reads from right to the left instead of left to right. Thus, for example, $P(43) = \{34\}$. This structure does not satisfy any of the properties P-1, P-2, or P-3.

Example 5 Define a *question* to be a function with a domain Ω. Let Q be a set of questions. In all states, the decision maker knows the answers to all the questions. To each question $q \in Q$, he obtains the answer $q(\omega)$. Assume that at each state, the decision maker excludes any state for which one of the questions will give an answer different from the answer obtained at that state. Thus, we have $P(\omega) = \{\omega' \mid q(\omega') = q(\omega)$ for all $q \in Q\}$. This information structure is partitional.

Example 6 (Awareness) Modify the previous example so that the set of questions, $Q(\omega)$, asked by the decision maker at ω varies with ω. Assume that the decision maker does not draw conclusions from the list of asked questions. Then, $P(\omega) = \{\omega' \mid q(\omega') = q(\omega)$ for all $q \in Q(\omega)\}$. This information structure satisfies P-1 but not necessarily P-2.

Example 7 (Selective Memory) A student gets the pass/fail results of an exam. He "forgets" bad news and remembers good news. Thus, $\Omega = \{G, B\}$, $P(G) = \{G\}$, $P(B) = \{G, B\}$. This information structure satisfies P-1 and P-2; however, it does not satisfy P-3 ($G \in P(B)$, $B \in P(B)$ but $B \notin P(G)$). At B, the decision maker does not conclude that the state is B from the absence of knowledge of the good news.

Example 8 (Always Having a Clear Picture) Consider a decision maker who always forms a clear picture of the world, even when he does not have it. Such a decision maker is modeled by an information structure P, with the property that $P(\omega)$ is a singleton for all ω. Of course, the desire to always have such a picture of the world yields an information structure that almost always does not satisfy any of the three properties. Note that example 4 was a special case of this example, although the psychological motive was different.

3.3 The Set-Theoretical Definition of Knowledge

In the previous section, we discussed "inference making." We will now formulate the notion that a decision maker "knows the event E." The definition elaborated in this section is built upon the notion of an information structure presented in the previous section.

Let (Ω, P) be an information structure (not necessarily partitional). It is said that the event E *is known at* ω if the decision maker, at ω, is able to exclude all states that are not in E, that is, if $P(\omega) \subseteq E$.

This definition is less obvious than it seems. Its validity depends on the procedure by which the decision maker concludes that he knows E. The definition fits a procedure by which the determination of knowledge of E at ω is accomplished by reviewing all states *outside* E and concluding that E is known at ω if all states outside E can be excluded. On the other hand, consider a decision maker who when at ω gets to know that the state is in $P(\omega)$. It is not obvious that he will conclude that the state is in E when $E \supseteq P(\omega)$, since this requires the ability to understand that $P(\omega)$ implies E. Consider your relationship with a friend who occasionally calls you. Your attitude to his call depends on your assessment of his motives for making the call. It could happen that if you fully describe all the states, you would discover that he calls you only on those days when his boss is angry at him. Yet, it is not clear that whenever he does call you, you conclude that his boss was angry at him.

The definition of "knowledge at a state" induces a set-theoretical definition of the term "to know E." The statement "the decision maker knows E" is identified with all states in which E is known, that is, with the set $K(E) = \{\omega\colon P(\omega) \subseteq E\}$. This formula, with a function P, defines the operator K, on subsets of Ω. If P is a partition, then $K(E)$ is the union of those cells in the partition that are contained in E. Because $K(E)$ is an event, the set $K(K(E))$ is also well defined and is interpreted as "the decision maker knows that he knows E." This interpretation is awkward since the meaning of a sentence like "I know that I know that I don't know E" in the natural language is questionable.

The definition of the operator K implies, without any assumptions on the information structure, the following properties:

K-0 If $E \subseteq F$, then $K(E) \subseteq K(F)$

Proof If $E \subseteq F$ and $\omega \in K(E)$, then $P(\omega) \subseteq E$ and thus $P(\omega) \subseteq F$ and hence $\omega \in K(F)$.

K-0' $K(E \cap F) = K(E) \cap K(F)$

Proof $\omega \in K(E \cap F)$ iff $P(\omega) \subseteq E \cap F$ iff both $P(\omega) \subseteq E$ and $P(\omega) \subseteq F$ iff $\omega \in K(E) \cap K(F)$.

K-0″ $K(\Omega) = \Omega$.

Additional properties of the operator K are derived from assumptions about the information structure. The following three properties, K-1,2,3 (entitled the axiom of knowledge, the axiom of transparency, and the axiom of wisdom, respectively) correspond to the three assumptions P-1,2,3.

K-1 $K(E) \subseteq E$.
This is interpreted as "the decision maker knows that E happens only when E happens." To see that P-1 implies K-1, let $\omega \in K(E)$; by definition, $P(\omega) \subseteq E$; by P-1, $\omega \in P(\omega)$ and thus $\omega \in E$.

K-2 $K(E) \subseteq K(K(E))$
This means that knowledge of E implies knowledge of the knowledge of E. To see that P-2 implies K-2, assume that $\omega \in K(E)$. We need to show that $\omega \in K(K(E))$, that is, $P(\omega) \subseteq K(E)$. Let $\omega' \in P(\omega)$. Then, by P-2, $P(\omega') \subseteq P(\omega)$. Because $\omega \in K(E)$, then, by definition of $K(E)$, $P(\omega) \subseteq E$ and thus $P(\omega') \subseteq E$ and hence $\omega' \in K(E)$.

K-3 $-K(E) \subseteq K(-K(E))$
This has the interpretation that "the decision maker is aware of what he does not know." If he does not know E, then he knows that he does not know E. The proof that P-3 implies K-3 is left as an exercise.

Note that K-1 and K-3 imply K-2; by K-1 and K-3, for any event E, $-K(E) = K(-K(E))$ and thus also $K(E) = -K(-K(E))$ and hence, substituting $-K(E)$ for E, $K(-K(E)) = -K(-K(-K(E)))$. These imply $K(E) = -K(-K(E)) = K(-K(-K(E))) = K(K(E))$.

3.4 Kripke's Model

Let us go back to the interpretation of a state. A state is usually thought of as a "full *description* of the world." The meaning of the term "description" depends on the language used, but the model of information structures discussed in the previous section does not allow us to talk explicitly about language. In contrast, Kripke's model of knowledge is based on a precise definition of language.

Following is a short presentation of Kripke's model, using the tools of mathematical logic. We start with the notion of a *language;* this consists of a set of formulas, each of which is a potential fact that the decision maker relates to as "true" or "false." Let Φ be a set of symbols, called "atomic propositions." A *formula* is a member of the smallest set L satisfying:

- All elements in Φ are in L.
- If ϕ is in L, then $(-\phi)$ is in L.
- If ϕ and ψ are in L, so are $(\phi \rightarrow \psi)$, $(\phi \wedge \psi)$ and $(\phi \vee \psi)$.
- If ϕ is in L, so is $(K(\phi))$.

Denote by $L(\Phi)$ the set of formulas. We sometimes omit parentheses to simplify the reading of the formulas.

A Kripke structure is a triple (Ω, π, P) where:

Ω is a set; its elements are called states.

$\pi: \Omega \times \Phi \rightarrow \{T, F\}$ is a truth assignment to every atomic proposition in Φ at every state in Ω. $\pi(\omega, \phi) = T$ means that the atomic proposition ϕ is assigned by π the value T at the state ω.

P is a function that assigns to every state ω a subset of Ω, with the same interpretation as in the set-theoretic model: $\omega' \in P(\omega)$ means that ω' is feasible (is not excluded) in ω.

Thus the primitives of the model comprise the set of atomic propositions that are true for each state, as well as a function that assigns to each state the set of states that are not excluded from being possible.

We now define the notion that "a formula ϕ is satisfied by a structure $M = (\Omega, \pi, P)$ at state ω," denoted by $(M,\omega) \models \phi$. The definition is inductive because the notion of a formula is defined inductively:

If ϕ is atomic then $(M, \omega) \models \phi$ if $\pi(\omega, \phi) = T$.

If $\phi = \neg\psi$, then $(M, \omega) \models \phi$ if not $(M, \omega) \models \psi$.

If $\phi = \psi_1 \wedge \psi_2$ then $(M, \omega) \models \phi$ if $(M, \omega) \models \psi_1$ and $(M, \omega) \models \psi_2$.

If $\phi = \psi_1 \vee \psi_2$ then $(M, \omega) \models \phi$ if $(M, \omega) \models \psi_1$ or $(M, \omega) \models \psi_2$.

If $\phi = \psi_1 \rightarrow \psi_2$ then $(M, \omega) \models \phi$ if either not $(M, \omega) \models \psi_1$ or $(M, \omega) \models \psi_2$.

If $\phi = K(\psi)$ then $(M, \omega) \models \phi$ if for all $\omega' \in P(\omega)$, we have $(M, \omega') \models \psi$.

The last condition is the main point of the model. It entails a systematic method for assigning truth values to the members of $L(\Phi)$ in a way that captures the intuition about what is knowledge. The content of the statement "the agent knows ψ at ω" is taken to mean that "ψ is true in all states that are not excluded by the agent at ω."

The above definitions imply the following claims without making any assumptions about the function P (their proofs are left as an exercise):

Claim 0   for all (M, ω), we have $(M, \omega) \models (K\phi \wedge K(\phi \rightarrow \psi)) \rightarrow K\psi$

Claim 0′   for all (M, ω), we have $(M, \omega) \models (K\phi \wedge K\psi) \rightarrow K(\phi \wedge \psi)$

Claim 0″   for all M, if $(M, \omega) \models \phi$ for all ω then $(M, \omega) \models K\phi$ for all ω.

These claims demonstrate that there are major aspects of bounded rationality regarding knowledge that cannot be captured by the model. Claim 0″ means that by definition, a fact that is true in all states of the world must be known by the decision maker at each state. In particular, the decision maker is capable of making unlimited logical inferences. The definition of satisfaction of a formula does not distinguish between more or less complicated formulas, and thus we are unable to model the possibility that knowledge of a proposition depends on its complexity.

The next proposition connects properties of the information structure P to the truth of formulas involving the knowledge symbol "K":

Proposition 3.2 For any formula ϕ:

1. If P satisfies P-1, then $(M, \omega) \models K\phi \to \phi$ for all (M, ω)

2. If P satisfies P-2, then $(M, \omega) \models K\phi \to K(K\phi)$ for all (M, ω)

3. If P satisfies P-3, then $(M, \omega) \models -K\phi \to K(-K\phi)$ for all (M, ω)

Proof The proofs are rather simple. The following is the proof of (1) (the proofs of (2) and (3) are valuable exercises):

By the definition of the satisfaction of an "implication formula" at (M, ω), $K\phi \to \phi$ is not satisfied at (M, ω) only if $(M, \omega) \models K\phi$ but not $(M, \omega) \models \phi$. This is impossible because $(M, \omega) \models K\phi$ requires that $(M, \omega') \models \phi$ for all $\omega' \in P(\omega)$; and because P satisfies P-1, it must be that $(M, \omega) \models \phi$. $\square$

The term "full description" is now well defined. We can think about a state in this model as the set of all formulas that are true at that state. What set of formulas, then, can be a "full description of the world"? It is impossible that both ϕ and $-\phi$ will be included in such a set. Proposition 3.2 demonstrated some other necessary constraints on a set of formulas to be the set of all formulas true at some state in some model. The constraints depend on additional assumptions on the information structure. The stronger the assumptions made on the information structure, the more constraints there are on what may be a feasible "full description of the world."

Let us conclude this section with a short comparison between Kripke's model and the set-theoretical model. Both include the primitive of an information structure (a P function). The basic difference lies in the fact that Kripke's model is more explicit regarding the definition of a state. To clarify the exact connection between the two models, let ϕ be a formula. The event $E_\phi = \{\omega \mid (M, \omega) \models \phi\}$ is the set of all states in which ϕ is true. We will see now that $E_{K\phi} = K(E_\phi)$; that is, every state in which $K\phi$ is satisfied by Kripke's model is a state where E_ϕ is known in the set-theoretical model of knowledge and vice versa. Formally:

$\omega \in E_{K\phi}$ iff (by definition of $E_{K\phi}$)

$(M, \omega) \models K\phi$ iff (by definition of $(M, \omega) \models K\phi$)

$(M, \omega') \models \phi$ for all $\omega' \in P(\omega)$ iff (by definition of E_ϕ)

$E_\phi \supseteq P(\omega)$ iff (by definition of $K(E_\phi)$)

$\omega \in K(E_\phi)$.

3.5 The Impact of the Timing of Decisions and Having More Information

We return now to decision theory. We will discuss two issues:

Timing of Decisions

In situations in which the decision maker anticipates obtaining information before taking an action, one can distinguish between two timings of decision making:

1. Ex-ante decision making. A decision is made before the information is revealed, and it is contingent on the content of the information to be received.

2. Ex-post decision making. The decision maker waits until the information is received and then makes a decision.

In standard decision problems, with fully rational decision makers, this distinction does not make any difference.

Having More Information

Basic intuition tells us that having more information is an advantage for the decision maker. Exceptional circumstances are often discussed in applied game theory. In a game, it may occur that not having access to some information is a blessing for a player. Sometimes player 1's lack of information may "guarantee" that he will not take a certain action, whereas without this guarantee, in order to avoid player 1's action, player 2 would have taken a preventive action that is harmful to player 1.

We will see now that the two properties, "making decisions ex-post and ex-ante are equivalent" and "the advantage of having more information," do not necessarily hold once we allow nonpartitional information structures. But, first we need some additional formal notions.

A *decision problem (with imperfect information)* is a tuple (A, Ω, P, u, π) where:

1. A is a set of actions

2. (Ω, P) is an information structure

3. u is a utility function on $A \times \Omega$

4. π is a probability measure on Ω. For simplicity, we assume that $\pi(\omega) > 0$ for all ω.

Let $\mathbf{P} = \{Z \mid \text{there is an } \omega \text{ so that } Z = P(\omega)\}$. If P is partitional, $\mathbf{P}$ is a partition. A *decision rule* is a function that assigns a unique action $a(Z) \in A$ to every $Z \in \mathbf{P}$. Thus, a decision maker is required to choose the same action in any two states, ω and ω', for which $P(\omega) = P(\omega')$.

A decision rule is *ex-ante optimal* if it maximizes $\Sigma_\omega u(a(P(\omega)), \omega)\pi(\omega)$. A decision rule is *ex-post optimal* if, for every set Z in the range of P, the action $a(Z)$ maximizes $\Sigma_\omega u(a, \omega)\pi(\omega \mid Z)$ where $\pi(\omega \mid Z)$ is the conditional probability of ω given Z. The information structure P is *finer than* P' if for all ω, $P(\omega) \subseteq P'(\omega)$.

The next two propositions show the validity of the above two properties for partitional information structures.

Proposition 3.3 Let P be a partitional information structure. A decision rule is ex-ante optimal iff it is ex-post optimal.

Proof This follows from the identity:

$$\Sigma_\omega u(a(P(\omega)), \omega)\pi(\omega) = \Sigma_{E \in P}\Sigma_{\omega \in E}u(a(E), \omega)\pi(\omega)$$
$$= \Sigma_{E \in P}\pi(E)[\Sigma_{\omega \in E}u(a(E), \omega)\pi(\omega \mid E)]. \ \square$$

Proposition 3.4 Let P and P' be two partitional information structures in which P is finer than P'. Then, the (ex-ante) expected utility of an ex-post maximizer of the problem (A, Ω, P, u, π) is at least as large as the (ex-ante) expected utility of an ex-post maximizer of (A, Ω, P', u, π).

Proof By Proposition 3.3 it is sufficient to note that the *ex-ante* maximizer of the problem (A, Ω, P, u, π) is at least as good as the *ex-ante* maximizer of (A, Ω, P', u, π). This follows from the fact that any decision rule that is feasible for the problem (A, Ω, P', u, π) is also feasible for the problem (A, Ω, P, u, π). $\square$

Comment Consider the model with the requirement that the description of a state ω includes a specification for each $\omega \in \Omega$ of an action $a(\omega)$ to be taken by the decision maker, without requiring that a unique action be assigned to every set in the information partition. A sensible definition of ex-post optimality is that for every ω, $a(\omega)$ is optimal given $P(\omega)$. With this definition, it is not true that "having more information" cannot hurt. To see this point, let Ω be a set which includes three equally likely states, ω_1, ω_2 and ω_3; let the set of actions be $\{x, y, z, n\}$; and let the utility function be displayed by the following table:

state	ω_1	ω_2	ω_3
action			
x	3	0	0
y	0	3	0
z	0	0	3
n	−3	2	2

Compare the decision problem with the partitional information structure P that induces the partition $\{\{\omega_1\}, \{\omega_2, \omega_3\}\}$, with the decision problem with the degenerate information structure P' for which $P'(\omega) \equiv \Omega$ for all ω.

Consider first the decision problem with P': The action function a', defined by $a'(\omega_1) = x$, $a'(\omega_2) = y$, and $a'(\omega_3) = z$, is optimal because for any state ω, the action $a'(\omega)$ yields an expected utility of 3 and is optimal given the decision maker's belief that any state is equally likely to be the one he is at.

Consider now the finer partition P. The unique ex-post maximizer is $a(\omega_1) = x$ and $a(\{\omega_2, \omega_3\}) = n$, which yields an ex-ante expected utility of only 7/3!

We now come to the main point of this section. When we depart from the assumption that the information structure is partitional, propositions 3.3 and 3.4 are no longer true, as the following example shows. A seller offers a risk-neutral decision maker a bet, asserting that acceptance will yield the decision maker $3 if the state is ω_2 and −$2 if either of the other states, ω_1 or ω_3, occurs. All three states are equally likely. If no additional information is given to the buyer, the best option for him is to reject the offer. However, to persuade the decision maker to accept the unfair offer, the seller commits to supplying the decision maker with the following "bonus" information. If the state is ω_1, the decision maker is told that ω_3 has not occurred; if the state is ω_3, the decision maker is told that ω_1 has not occurred. If the decision maker does not understand the rule by which the bonus information is given, this information, although true, distorts the decision maker's beliefs so that, when given the information, he always prefers to take the bet.

The phenomenon exhibited here is quite common. It corresponds to all kind of situations where the decision maker gets information about the state of the world from an "interested party" without taking into account the source of information. If the decision maker takes note of the motivation behind the supply of information, he escapes from the trap; if he does not make these inferences, the additional information he obtains may worsen his situation.

Formally, let $\Omega = \{\omega_1, \omega_2, \omega_3\}$, with $\pi(\omega) = 1/3$ for all ω and $A = \{n, y\}$. The utility function $u(a, \omega)$ and the information structures P and P' are displayed in the following table:

	ω_1	ω_2	ω_3
n	0	0	0
y	−2	3	−2
P	$\{\omega_1, \omega_2\}$	$\{\omega_2\}$	$\{\omega_3, \omega_2\}$
P'	Ω	Ω	Ω

For the decision problem (A, Ω, P', u, π), the ex-ante and the ex-post optimal decision rule is $a' \equiv n$, obtaining an expected payoff of 0. The structure P is finer than P'. The ex-post optimizer for (A, Ω, P, u, π) is $a \equiv y$, obtaining the ex-ante expected utility of $-1/3$. Thus, although the information structure P is finer than P', it induces a decision rule that is, on average, worse.

The decision problem (A, Ω, P, u, π) demonstrates the difference between ex-post and ex-ante optimality. The ex-post optimizer is $a(\omega) \equiv y$, which, of course, is different from the unique ex-ante optimizer $a(\{\omega_1, \omega_2\}) = n$, $a(\{\omega_2\}) = y$, and $a(\{\omega_3, \omega_2\}) = n$.

Comment Note a delicate point in the interpretation of the comparison between two different information structures with the same state space. If a state is a full description of the situation, then there is only one information structure associated with one state space. We need to adjust slightly the notion "P is finer than P'" in order to cope with this problem.

3.6 On the Possibility of Speculative Trade

Speculative trade is an exchange of goods not motivated either by different tastes regarding the exchanged goods or by different atti-

tudes toward risk; rather, it is an outcome of differences in information. Take, for example, the case where agent 1 holds a lottery
ticket, L, and agent 2 may be interested in buying it for the price α.
Assume that both are risk-neutral. Of course, trade is possible if the
two agents have different assessments of the underlying probabilities that determine L's payoff. But an intriguing question is
whether such a trade is possible when the two agents

1. have the same prior beliefs on the uncertain elements

2. have different information

3. have a mutual understanding of the information structures

4. take their partner's willingness to trade into consideration. That
is, before agreeing to trade, each trader makes the right inference
from the willingness of the other trader to trade.

Point 4 is somewhat vague. Does agent 1 make the inference from
the willingness of agent 2 to trade with or without taking into
account agent 2's considerations concerning agent 1's willingness
to trade? For a precise formalization of point 4, we need the concept
of common knowledge. The concept has been extensively explored
in the last two decades. The following is a very short introduction
to the topic.

A Short Detour to the Concept of Common Knowledge

One definition of common knowledge, suggested by Lewis, was
formulated by Aumann using the set-theoretical model of knowledge. Let Ω be the state space and K_1 and K_2 be two knowledge
functions (that is, $K_i(E)$ is the set of states in which i "knows that E
occurs") representing the knowledge of two agents, 1 and 2, but
not necessarily satisfying the properties of "fully rational knowledge." An event E is *common knowledge*, between 1 and 2, in the
state ω if ω is a member of all sets of the type $K_1(E)$, $K_2(E)$, $K_1(K_2(E))$,
$K_2(K_1(E))$, and so on.

Example Consider the following two partitions of $\Omega = \{\omega_1, \omega_2, \omega_3, \omega_4, \omega_5, \omega_6, \omega_7, \omega_8\}$:

$P_1 = \{\{\omega_1, \omega_2\}, \{\omega_3, \omega_4, \omega_5\}, \{\omega_6\}, \{\omega_7, \omega_8\}\}$

$P_2 = \{\{\omega_1\}, \{\omega_2, \omega_3, \omega_4\}, \{\omega_5\}, \{\omega_6, \omega_7\}, \{\omega_8\}\}$ and the set $E = \{\omega_1, \omega_2, \omega_3, \omega_4\}$.

The set E is not common knowledge in any state ω. Verify this by the chain calculation:

$K_1(E) = \{\omega_1, \omega_2\}$ and $K_2(E) = E$,

$K_2(K_1(E)) = \{\omega_1\}$ and $K_1(K_2(E)) = \{\omega_1, \omega_2\}$,

$K_1(K_2(K_1(E))) = \varnothing$ and $K_2(K_1(K_2(E))) = \{\omega_1\}$.

The set $F = \{\omega_1, \omega_2, \omega_3, \omega_4, \omega_5\}$ (or any set that includes F) is common knowledge in any of the states in F because for both i, $K_i(F) = F$; thus $K_i K_j K_i \ldots K_i(F) = K_i K_j K_i \ldots K_j(F) = F$.

Note that underlying this definition of common knowledge is the assumption that each agent understands the information structures of both agents. For example, at ω_1, agent 2 bases his knowledge that agent 1 knows E on his understanding that both $P_1(\omega_1)$ and $P_1(\omega_2)$ are subsets of E.

Define an event E to be *self-evident* for the information structures P_1 and P_2 if, for all $\omega \in E$ and for both i, $P_i(\omega) \subseteq E$. In other words, a self-evident event is an event such that whenever it occurs, the two agents know that it occurs. The following proposition provides an alternative definition for common knowledge that is equivalent to the previous one, as long as property P-1 ($\omega \in P_i(\omega)$ for all ω) is satisfied by the two information structures, P_1 and P_2.

Proposition 3.5 Assume that P_1 and P_2 are information structures satisfying P-1. Let K_1 and K_2 be the knowledge functions induced from P_1 and P_2, respectively. The set E^* is common knowledge at ω if and only if it includes a self-evident set E containing ω.

Proof Assume that there is a self-evident event E so that $\omega \in E \subseteq E^*$. By the definition of a self-evident event, for both i, $E \subseteq K_i(E)$ and, by P-1, $K_i(E) \subseteq E$; thus $K_i(E) = E$ for both i, which implies that $K_i K_j \ldots K_i(E) = K_i K_j \ldots K_j(E) = E$. By K-0, since $E \subseteq E^*$ we have $K_i(E) \subseteq K_i(E^*)$ *and thus* $E = K_i K_j \ldots K_i(E) \subseteq K_i K_j \ldots K_i(E^*)$ and $E = K_i K_j \ldots K_j(E) \subseteq K_i K_j \ldots K_j(E^*)$. Hence, since $\omega \in E$, ω is a member of all sets of the type $K_i K_j \ldots K_i(E^*)$ and $K_i K_j \ldots K_j(E^*)$. That is, E^* is common knowledge at ω.

Conversely, if E^* is common knowledge at ω, take E to be the intersection of all sets of the type $K_i K_j \ldots K_i(E^*)$ and $K_i K_j \ldots K_j(E^*)$. Because E^* is common knowledge at ω, $\omega \in E$. By K-1, which follows from P-1, $E \subseteq E^*$. To show that E is a self-evident event, one just has to verify that for any $\omega \in E$, $P_i(\omega) \subseteq E$. This follows from the fact that because $\omega \in E$, ω belongs to any set of the form $K_i K_j \ldots K_i(E^*)$. $\square$

We are ready to return to the speculative trade question. Is it possible that two agents, 1 and 2,

1. have the same prior beliefs on Ω,

2. have different information structures, P_1 and P_2,

3. have a mutual understanding of the information structures, and

4. share common knowledge at some ω that agent 1 believes that the expectation of a given lottery L is strictly above α and that agent 2 believes that the expectation of the lottery L is strictly below α?

If the answer is positive, then at ω, an exchange of the lottery L for α is acceptable for the two agents even after they both consider taking the willingness to trade as an additional signal that may modify their knowledge.

The answer to the above question is negative if the information structures are partitional; consequently, "speculative trade" cannot be explained as an outcome of different information structures.

Proposition 3.6 Assume that both information structures, (Ω, P_1) and (Ω, P_2), are partitional. Let L be a lottery on the space Ω. Then, it is never common knowledge between the two agents that agent 1 believes that the expectation of the lottery L is above α and that agent 2 believes that the expectation of the lottery L is below α.

Proof Assume that the event $E^* = \{\omega \mid$ agent 1 evaluates the lottery L above α and agent 2 evaluates it below $\alpha\}$ is common knowledge at some state ω^*. Then, there is a self-evident event E so that $\omega^* \in E \subseteq E^*$, and since $P_i(\omega) \subseteq E$, for all $\omega \in E$, we have $E = \cup_{\omega \in E} P_i(\omega)$. Because P_i is partitional, for each i, $\{P_i(\omega)\}_{\omega \in E}$ is a collection of disjoint sets. For each $\omega \in E$, the expected value of L, given $P_1(\omega)$, is above α and thus $Ex(L \mid E) > \alpha$. Similarly, for each $\omega \in E$, the expected value of L given $P_2(\omega)$ is below α and thus $Ex(L \mid E) < \alpha$, a contradiction. $\square$

However, the impossibility of speculative trade does not necessarily hold if the information structure does not satisfy property P-3. Consider the space $\Omega = \{\omega_1, \omega_2, \omega_3\}$ and a probability measure π, that assigns equal probabilities to the three states. Assume

$P_1(\omega) \equiv \{\omega_1, \omega_2, \omega_3\}$ and

$P_2(\omega_1) = \{\omega_1, \omega_2\}$, $P_2(\omega_2) = \{\omega_2\}$ and $P_2(\omega_3) = \{\omega_2, \omega_3\}$.

Both P_1 and P_2 satisfy properties P-1 and P-2, but P_2 does not satisfy P-3. Let L be the lottery $L(\omega_2) = 1$, and $L(\omega_1) = L(\omega_3) = 0$, and let $\alpha = 0.35$. For all ω, agent 1 believes that the expectation of L is $1/3$ (which is strictly less than 0.35), and agent 2 believes that the expectation of L is 0.5 or 1 (which are strictly above 0.35). Thus, for any state ω, it is common knowledge that agent 1 is ready to sell L for 0.35 and that agent 2 is ready to pay this price. Thus, the absence of a fully rational treatment of knowledge allows speculative trade.

3.7 Bibliographic Notes

The chapter began with the basic models of knowledge. The discussion of the set-theoretical model in Section 2 is based on Geanakoplos (1989) (see also Hintikka (1962)).

Section 3 dwells on Kripke's model, which was developed in the late 1950s. An excellent presentation of the material is found in Fagin, Halpern, Moses, and Vardi (1995). The comparison between Kripke's model and the set-theoretical model is based on their presentation.

Geanakoplos (1989) is the source of much of the discussion in Section 4.

Section 5 is based on Geanakoplos (1992) and (1994). Two classic works on the notion of common knowledge are Lewis (1969) and Aumann (1976). For work on speculative trade and common knowledge, see Milgrom and Stokey (1982).

3.8 Projects

1. *Innovative* In this chapter, we discussed the notion of knowledge. Consider other operators like: "I believe that," "I am pleased that," "it is impossible that," and so on. For each of these operators, assess the meaning of the sentence $K(K\phi)$ and check the validity of the propositions

$K\phi \land K(\phi \to \psi) \to K\psi$

$K\phi \to \phi$

$K\phi \to K(K\phi)$

$-K\phi \to K(-K\phi)$.

2. *Exercise* (Based on Geanakoplos [1994].) The following is another model of knowledge. The primitives of the model are Ω, a set of states, and K, a function that assigns to each event E a subset of states $K(E)$, interpreted as the set of states in which E is known. The following is a natural way to construct an "equivalent" information structure (Ω, P) from the model (Ω, K) so that $K(E) = \{\omega \mid P(\omega) \subseteq E\}$. Given a function K, define $P(\omega) = \cap_{\{E \mid \omega \in K(E)\}} E$. The idea of the construction is that at ω, the decision maker excludes any state ω' that does not belong to all known events. Show that if K satisfies K-0 and K-0', then $K(E) = \{\omega \mid P(\omega) \subseteq E\}$. Furthermore, for any $i = 1, 2, 3$, the induced function P satisfies property P-i if the function K satisfies property K-i.

3. *Innovative* As we emphasized, the models of knowledge we discussed do not specify the process by which the knowledge is acquired. Invent some scenarios that will include a specification of the method by which knowledge is acquired and investigate the properties of knowledge satisfied by those processes. Consult Lipman (1995b).

4. *Reading* Discuss the problem of Ulysses and the sirens in light of the material presented in this chapter. See Geanakoplos (1992) and Elster (1979).

5. *Exercise* (Based on Rubinstein and Wolinsky (1990).) Let Ω be a finite space of states. Let P_1 and P_2 be two information structures. Let F be the set of functions that are defined over the set of subsets of Ω and assign to every subset of Ω either the value "True" (denoted by T) or the value "Not True." We say that $f \in F$ is *preserved under disjoint union* if for all disjoint sets R and S such that $f(R) = T$ and $f(S) = T$, we have $f(R \cup S) = T$. We say that f is *preserved under difference* if for all R and S such that $R \supseteq S$, $f(R) = T$, and $f(S) = T$, we also have $f(R - S) = T$. Prove and provide applications for the proposition that if P_1 and P_2 satisfy conditions P-1 and P-2 and f and g are two functions in F such that

1. there is no S for which $f(S) = g(S) = T$,

2. f and g are preserved under disjoint union,

3. f and g are preserved under difference,

then, there is no ω^* at which the set $\{\omega \mid f(P_1(\omega)) = T$ and $g(P_2(\omega)) = T\}$ is common knowledge.

4   Modeling Limited Memory

4.1   Imperfect Recall

Memory is a special type of knowledge. It is what a decision maker knows at a certain date about what he knew at a previous date. Imperfect recall is a particular case of imperfection of knowledge that lies at the heart of human processing of information. In this chapter, we discuss some of the major differences between a decision problem with perfect recall and one with imperfect recall. We will see that some basic properties that hold for decision problems with perfect recall fail to hold with imperfect recall. We will also question whether the model commonly used to discuss imperfect recall is appropriate for modeling this phenomenon.

The common interpretation of a decision problem with imperfect recall refers to a situation in which an individual has to carry out several successive actions but faces memory limits. When the decision maker is an organization consisting of agents who possibly act at different instances, the concept of imperfect recall may reflect communication problems arising between the agents.

Note that placing constraints on the strategies of economic agents, especially stationarity, which may be interpreted as expressing imperfect recall, is common in economics and game theory. Usually, these limits result from difficulties in "solving" the model and are not expressions of plausible assumptions about the decision makers. The phenomena discussed in this chapter have been avoided in the standard economic literature by assumptions like the "stationarity of the environment" that guarantee that forgetting will be harmless as long as all the agents recall the same information.

4.2   An Extensive Decision Making Model with Imperfect Information

The standard framework to discuss decision making with imperfect recall is the model of an extensive decision problem, which is a conventional extensive game with one player. An extensive decision problem is usually thought of as a description of the order of the decisions that the decision maker may confront in the course of the situation analyzed. In addition to the order of moves, the model spells out the knowledge the decision maker obtains at each instance at which he is required to move.

A (finite) *decision problem* (with imperfect information) is a five-tuple $\Gamma = (H, C, \rho, u, I)$ where:

1. H is a finite set of *histories*. We assume that the empty sequence, $\varnothing$, is an element of H and that if $(a_1, \ldots, a_t) \in H$ and $(a_1, \ldots, a_t) \neq \varnothing$, then $(a_1, \ldots, a_{t-1}) \in H$.

We interpret a history $(a_1, \ldots, a_t) \in H$ as a possible sequence of actions that can be taken by the decision maker or by chance. When presenting a decision problem diagrammatically, we draw H as a tree whose nodes are the set of histories with root $\varnothing$, and each of whose edges connects a node $(a_1, \ldots, a_t)$ with a node $(a_1, \ldots, a_{t+1})$.

The history $(a_1, \ldots, a_t) \in H$ is *terminal* if there is no $(a_1, \ldots, a_t, a) \in H$. The set of terminal histories is denoted by Z. The set of actions available to the decision maker or to chance, following a nonterminal history h, is $A(h) = \{a \mid (h, a) \in H\}$. We assume that $A(h)$ contains at least two elements.

2. C is a subset of $H - Z$. Chance (that is, elements outside the control of the decision maker) determines the way the situation progresses at each history in C.

3. ρ is the decision maker's belief about the chance player's behavior. ρ assigns a probability measure on $A(h)$ to each history $h \in C$. We assume that $\rho(h)(a)$ is strictly positive for all $h \in C$ and $a \in A(h)$.

4. $u: Z \to \mathbf{R}$ is a utility function that assigns a number (payoff) to each of the terminal histories. In any case where the decision maker has to choose among lotteries over the terminal histories, we assume that he behaves as an expected payoff maximizer.

Thus, the set of histories H is partitioned into three subsets:

Z: the set of terminal histories;

C: the set of histories after which the chance player moves;

$D = H - Z - C$: the set of histories after which the decision maker moves.

When the decision maker is about to move, he knows he is at one of the histories in D, but the model allows him not to recognize the exact history where he is. We adopt the previous chapter's approach and formulate knowledge as an information structure on the set D.

5. I, the set of information sets, is a partition of D. It is assumed that for all h, h' in the same cell of the partition, $A(h) = A(h')$, that is, the sets of actions available to the decision maker at all the histories in the same information set are identical.

We interpret the partition of D into information sets as a description of the knowledge *provided* to the decision maker. Although the decision maker knows at which information set he is located, if the set is not a singleton, he is not *told* (although he may infer) which history led to it. If all the information sets are singletons, then we say that the decision problem has *perfect information*.

We now turn to the different notions of strategy. A *(pure) strategy*, f, is a function that assigns an element of $A(h)$ to every history $h \in D$ with the restriction that if h and h' are in the same information set, then $f(h) = f(h')$. Any pure strategy f leads to a distribution over the terminal nodes. For example, when there are no chance moves, this distribution assigns probability 1 to the history $(f(\varnothing), f(f(\varnothing)), f(f(\varnothing),f(f(\varnothing))), \dots)$.

Note that this definition of a strategy follows the game theoretic tradition and requires that the decision maker specify his actions after histories he will not reach if he follows the strategy. The more natural definition of a strategy is as a *plan of action:* a function that assigns an action only to histories reached with positive probability. Formally, f is a plan of action if there exists a subset of histories H' so that $f(h)$ is defined for all $h \in H'$ iff h is reached by f with positive probability. The game theoretic concept of a strategy can be interpreted as "notes" from a reasoning process (such as "backward induction") in which the decision maker needs to specify what he would do at histories he will not reach in order to determine that he will not indeed reach those histories.

In game theory, we often talk about two extensions of the notion of a strategy, each of which uses random factors: A *behavioral strategy*, b, is a function such that for all $h \in D$, $b(h)$ is a *distribution* over $A(h)$ such that $b(h) = b(h')$ for any two histories, h and h', that lie within the same information set. A *mixed strategy* is a distribution over the set of pure strategies. (Note that in some of the literature, a mixed strategy is defined as a distribution over behavioral strategies.)

Thus, a behavioral strategy is a rule of behavior that assigns (possibly random) behaviors to each of the information sets in the decision problem. These random elements represent stochastically independent factors. The element $b(h)$ is the "order" given by the decision maker to himself (or to an agent who acts on his behalf) specifying the random device to use whenever he is at h in order to determine the action that will be taken at h. If the decision problem does not rule out the possibility that the decision maker will be at the same information set more than once (we will call this "absent-mindedness"), then the random element in the behavioral strategy is realized independently at each instance in which the information set is visited. On the other hand, a mixed strategy is a rule of behavior that uses a random device only once, prior to the starting point of the problem. (As usual, the interpretation of the random device does not have to be, literally, of a roulette wheel or of a die. One can also take it as a rule of behavior that is dependent on external random elements.)

A behavioral strategy b leads to a distribution of terminal nodes. The strategy b^* is *optimal*, if no other behavioral strategy yields a higher expected utility. Thus, optimality is examined from the perspective of the point prior to the onset of the decision problem.

In Example 1 (fig. 4.1), the decision maker has eight pure strategies (and six plans of actions). A behavioral strategy for this decision maker is a triple of probabilities, one for each information set,

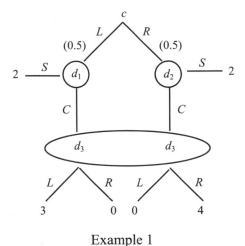

Example 1

Figure 4.1

and a mixed strategy is a lottery on the eight pure strategies. The unique optimal strategy is to choose S at d_1, C at d_2 and R at d_3.

4.3 Perfect and Imperfect Recall

Our understanding is that the knowledge expressed by the information partition I results from a decision maker's cognitive abilities. This knowledge is imposed on the decision maker by his senses. We use the term "to know ψ" as we did in the previous chapter. If ψ is true for all histories in a certain information set, we say that the decision maker at that information set knows ψ. In Example 1, at the information set $d_3 = \{(L, C), (R, C)\}$, the decision maker knows on one hand that he played C at the first stage since $d_3 \subseteq \{(a_1, a_2, \ldots, a_K) \mid a_2 = C\}$. On the other hand, at d_3, he does not know the chance move, which he did know at d_1 and d_2.

However, we sometimes talk about knowledge as it is perceived after the decision maker has made further inferences regarding where he is, which he makes on the basis of considerations such as the knowledge of the strategy he is using. Thus, if he has decided to play C at d_1 and S at d_2, at d_3 he may conclude that he is at (L, C). Therefore, we have to be careful and clarify the type of knowledge we are referring to whenever we use phrases involving knowledge.

We are now ready to approach the main definitions of this chapter, those of problems with perfect and imperfect recall. These concepts refer to knowledge as expressed by the information sets only. Define exp(h) to be the decision maker's experience along the history h, that is, the list of the information sets he encountered along the history and the actions he took at each of these information sets.

A decision problem with perfect recall is one in which exp(h) = exp(h') for any two histories, h, $h' \in D$, that lie in the same information set. (The condition of equality of the sequences exp(h) and exp(h') implies that the information sets appear in the same order in those sequences.) Thus, in a decision problem with perfect recall, the decision maker "remembers" the actions he took in the past and whatever information he obtained about chance moves. A decision problem that does not satisfy the above condition is called a decision problem with *imperfect recall*.

Example 1 is the most common example of imperfect recall. The decision maker perceives some valuable information at a certain stage, information that may be useful at a later stage, but he will not perceive this information later. More specifically, the decision maker can obtain the payoff 2 at date 1 or choose to make a choice at date 2 between L and R, which may yield a payoff lower or higher than 2. At the first date, "somebody" tells the decision maker what action he should take at date 2, but he will not remember the content of what he is told when he reaches the later date. Formally, the decision problem is of imperfect recall, because both histories, (L, C) and (R, C), are in d_3, but $\exp(L, C) = (\emptyset, \{L\}, C)$ while $\exp(R, C) = (\emptyset, \{R\}, C)$.

In Example 2 (fig. 4.2), the decision maker has to choose a password, L or R, and then he has to repeat it in order to achieve a non-zero payoff. If he repeats L twice, he gets 1; if he repeats R twice he gets 2 (that is, he has some reason to prefer using the password R rather than L). When the time comes to repeat the password, the decision maker knows that he has chosen a password but does not recall whether it is L or R. Formally, the problem is one with imperfect recall because $\exp(L) = (\emptyset, L) \neq \exp(R) = (\emptyset, R)$.

Example 3 is the least standard example. Consider an absent-minded driver who, in order to get home, has to take the highway and get off at the second exit. Turning at the first exit leads into a bad neighborhood (payoff 0). Turning at the second exit yields the highest reward (payoff 4). If he continues beyond the second exit, he will have to go a very long way before he can turn back home (payoff 1). The driver is absent-minded and is aware of this fact. When reaching an intersection, his senses do not tell him whether he is at the first or the second intersection; that is, he cannot remember how many he has passed. Here, the decision maker does

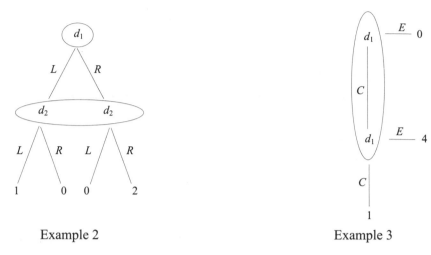

Example 2   Example 3

Figure 4.2

not distinguish between the history ϕ and the history (C); in particular, at (C), he forgets that he already took one action. This decision problem is an example of a decision problem *exhibiting absent-mindedness*; that is, the decision problem has an information set containing both a history h and a subhistory of h. Note that decision problems with absent-mindedness were ruled out in Kuhn's original formulation of extensive games.

At this point, we turn to a discussion of a series of properties that hold for decision problems with perfect recall yet fail to hold for general decision problems with imperfect recall. These properties are so elementary that they are seldom mentioned in the literature. They "justify" ignoring some potential procedural elements in the analysis of rational decision making.

4.4 Time Consistency

Our definition of optimality refers to ex-ante considerations, those arising before the decision problem is initiated. That is, the decision maker makes a plan, before the decision problem begins to unfold, regarding what to do in each possible scenario that may arise. But what happens if such a stage does not transpire and the decision maker makes his decisions as the situation unfolds? Or, if he does make a plan in advance, can he decide "not to decide" and to postpone his decisions regarding future events to another stage?

When we usually analyze conventional decision problems with perfect recall, these issues are ignored. The reason for this neglect is that they appear to be insignificant. Yet, we will see that these issues may be critical for the analysis of decision problems with imperfect recall. We will not address these issues directly; instead, we will analyze the property of time consistency whose absence makes them relevant.

In order to formalize the notion of time consistency, we need to describe the decision maker's belief updating method. A *belief* system is a function μ that assigns to any information set X and any history $h \in X$, a non-negative number $\mu(h \mid X)$ such that $\Sigma_{h \in X}\mu(h \mid X) = 1$. It has the interpretation that when arriving at X, the decision maker assigns the probability $\mu(h \mid X)$ to the possibility that he is actually at h. For decision problems with perfect recall, it is common to assume that the belief system must conform with the principles of Bayesian updating. Extending the principles of Bayesian updating to decision problems with absent-mindedness is not conceptually trivial. Here, we will follow one approach that generalizes Bayesian updating. Given a behavioral strategy b, a *consistent* belief system μ assigns to every information set X reached with a positive probability, and to every $h \in X$, a number, $\mu(h \mid X)$. This number is required to be the long-run proportion of instances at which a decision maker who follows b and "visits" the information set X, is at h out of the total number of "visits" in X. That is, for consistent μ, $\mu(h \mid X) = p(h \mid b)/\Sigma_{h' \in X}p(h' \mid b)$ where $p(h \mid b)$ is the probability of reaching the history h when employing the behavioral strategy b. Note that for any case that does not involve absent-mindedness, the consistency requirement is equivalent to Bayesian updating. With absent-mindedness the meaning of Bayesian updating is not clear and the requirement of consistency of beliefs extends beyond the Bayesian requirement. For instance, in Example 3, if the behavioral strategy selects C with probability of $1/2$, a consistent belief at d_1 assigns probability $2/3$ to being at the first intersection.

We say that a strategy is time-consistent if at no information set reached as the decision problem unfolds does reassessing the strategy for the remainder of the decision problem lead to a change in the plan of action. That is, a behavioral strategy b is *time-consistent* if there is a belief system μ consistent with b such that for every information set X that is reached with positive probability under b,

$$\Sigma_{h \in X}\mu(h)\Sigma_{z \in Z}p(z \mid h, b)u(z) \geq \Sigma_{h \in X}\mu(h)\Sigma_{z \in Z}p(z \mid h, b')u(z),$$

for any behavioral strategy b', where $p(z \mid h, b)$ is the probability of reaching the terminal history z when employing b, conditional on h having occurred.

Note that the definition of time-consistency does not make any requirement of optimality ex-ante. Nevertheless, a well-known fact about decision problems with perfect recall is that a strategy is optimal if and only if it is time-consistent. Actually, we can prove this equivalence for a larger set of decision problems. In order to state the result, we need one definition: A decision problem is said to satisfy condition (∗) if for any information set X and two histories h', $h'' \in X$ that split at $h \in C$, the information sets that appear in $\exp(h')$ are the same as in $\exp(h'')$. In other words, in any problem satisfying condition (∗), it is impossible for the decision maker to have different information regarding a chance move along two histories that lie in the same information set. Example 2 is a decision problem with no absent-mindedness, satisfying (∗). Example 1 does not satisfy this condition: The histories (L, C) and (R, C) are split by a move of chance but the list of information sets along the two histories is not the same. Of course, any problem with perfect recall satisfies condition (∗).

Proposition 4.1 Consider a decision problem without absent-mindedness that satisfies condition (∗). Then, a strategy is optimal if and only if it is time-consistent.

We will not prove this proposition here: we will make do with reviewing several problems with imperfect recall for which time consistency and optimality are not identical properties.

Consider Example 1. The optimal strategy is to choose S at d_1, C at d_2, and R at d_3. It yields an expected value of 3. However, upon reaching d_1, the decision maker, if he is able to review his strategy, would prefer changing it to C at d_1 and L at d_3. Thus, the optimal strategy here is not time-consistent.

Let us go back to the procedural aspects of decision making and see how these details influence the analysis of the situation.

Planning Stage If there is a planning stage at which the strategy is determined then the best expected payoff for the decision maker is 3. In contrast, in the absence of a planning stage prior to the beginning of the situation, then the decision maker does better as he is able to make superior plans about how to play at d_3 given the information that he has reached d_1 or d_2.

Postponing Decision If there is a planning stage and the decision maker is able to make a decision regarding when to decide about the move at d_3, he is better off if he postpones his decision regarding d_3 to d_1 or d_2.

The next example (fig. 4.3) shows that a strategy may be time-consistent but not optimal.

A decision maker has two opportunities to stop the game. Consider the strategy where the decision maker plays C at both information sets. The only belief consistent with this strategy assigns probability 1/2 to each of the histories in each of the information sets. The strategy always to continue is optimal at each of the information sets and thus is time-consistent. However, the optimal

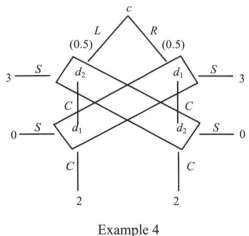

Example 4

Figure 4.3

strategy in this problem is to choose S in each of the information sets.

The strategy to play C at both information sets seems to describe a "bad equilibrium" prevailing in the decision maker's mind. In this example, if the decision maker does not have a planning stage before the chance player moves, he must form beliefs at one information set about what he would have done if he had reached the other information set. Believing at each information set that had he visited the other set, he would have chosen C is an "equilibrium" (even if the decision maker is able, at d_1, to control his future behavior at d_2 if it is reached).

For decision problems with absent-mindedness, the consistency problem is more severe. If the driver in Example 3 plans his trip in advance, he must conclude that it is impossible for him to get home and that he should not exit when he reaches an intersection. That is, his optimal plan is to choose C, yielding a payoff of 1. Now, suppose that he reaches an intersection. Should he remember his strategy, he would conclude that he is at the first intersection with probability $1/2$. Then, reviewing his plan, he would conclude that it is optimal for him to leave the highway since it yields an expected payoff of 2. Thus, despite no new information and no change in his preferences, the decision maker is tempted to change his initial plan once he reaches an intersection!

The driver's example has a certain paradoxical flavor owing to the conflict between two ways of reasoning at an intersection. The first instructs the decision maker to follow his initial decision not to exit, following an intuitive principle of rationality that unless new information is received or there is a change in tastes, previous decisions should not be changed. The second way of reasoning, maximizing the expected payoff given the belief, suggests he should deviate from his initial decision.

Note that this is not a standard economic example of time inconsistency. Usually, time inconsistency is obtained as a consequence of changes in preferences (tastes) during the execution of the optimal plan. Here, the inconsistency arises without any change in information or preferences.

4.5 The Role of Randomization

In standard decision theory, it is assumed that a decision maker uses a strategy that does not employ random devices. Two rationales underlie this assumption. First, people tend not to use such random devices. Second, for decision problems with perfect recall, even if a player is allowed to use a random device to determine his action at every history, he would not be able to obtain an expected payoff higher than what could be obtained without the random device.

Let us expand on the last point. We have mentioned two ways of using random devices, expressed by the notions of mixed and behavioral strategies. A mixed strategy induces a linear combination of the lotteries induced by pure strategies and thus (for problems with either perfect or imperfect recall), if the decision maker is an expected utility maximizer, a mixed strategy cannot induce a payoff strictly higher than the payoff to any pure strategy. However, can a behavioral strategy be better than any pure strategy?

Proposition 4.2 (Isbell (1957)) For any decision problem with no absent-mindedness, no behavioral strategy is strictly better than all pure strategies.

The idea of proof For a problem that does not exhibit absent-mindedness, the expected payoff is linear in the probability that is assigned to each action at every history; thus, for such a problem, it cannot be beneficial to use behavioral strategies.

In contrast, consider again the absent-minded driver example (Example 3). The optimal pure strategy is to choose C. However, the behavioral strategy in which the decision maker equally mixes the two actions yields the higher expected payoff of 1.25. The optimal behavioral strategy is actually to choose C with the probability p that maximizes $p^2 + 4p(1 - p)$. That is, the optimal strategy is $p = 2/3$, yielding an expected payoff of $4/3$.

The above example is not coincidental. One can show that:

Proposition 4.3 For any four-tuple (H, C, ρ, I) with absent-mindedness, there is a payoff function u so that for the decision problem (H, C, ρ, I, u) there exists a behavioral strategy strictly better than all pure strategies.

Thus, the question whether or not a decision maker considers the use of random devices is crucial only for the analysis of decision problems with absent-mindedness.

Note that the time inconsistency in the absent-minded driver example persists when we allow the decision maker to choose behavioral strategies. Given his optimal behavioral strategy of not exiting with probability $2/3$, let α be the probability he assigns to "being at the first intersection." Then, on reviewing his plan, he should maximize $\alpha[p^2 + 4(1 - p)p] + (1 - \alpha)[p + 4(1 - p)]$, where p is the probability of not exiting, and conclude that the optimal p is $\max\{0, (7\alpha - 3)/6\alpha\}$. This is inconsistent with his original plan unless $\alpha = 1$. In other words, his original plan is time-consistent if and only if he holds the unreasonable belief (given his strategy) that there is no chance that he has passed the first intersection. Consistent beliefs must assign a probability to the second intersection that is $2/3$ times the probability assigned to the first intersection, that is, $\alpha = 0.6$. Actually, the only strategy that satisfies the consistency requirement here is $p = 4/9$ (the solution of the equations $\alpha = 1/(1 + p)$ and $(7\alpha - 3)/6\alpha = p$).

The Equivalence Between Behavioral and Mixed Strategies

A consequence of the Kuhn (1953) theorem is that for any decision problem with perfect recall, a distribution over the terminal histories can be induced from a mixed strategy if and only if it can be induced by a behavioral strategy.

We have already seen that with imperfect recall, a behavioral strategy may be better than all mixed strategies; thus, not all behavioral strategies can be mimicked by mixed strategies. We will show now that in decision problems with imperfect recall, it can also occur that a mixed strategy may not be mimicked by a behavioral strategy. This is insignificant for decision makers who are expected utility maximizers; in such a case, no mixed strategy is better than any pure strategy. But once we move to other theories of decision under uncertainty (like maxminimization), this fact is significant.

Consider Example 2 once again. The mixed strategy $1/2[L, L] + 1/2[R, R]$ induces the distribution $(1/2, 0, 0, 1/2)$ on Z. However, a behavioral strategy $((p, 1 - p), (q, 1 - q))$ induces a distribution that places probability 0 on (L, R) only if $p(1 - q) = 0$, that is, only if either $p = 0$ or $q = 1$, in which case the probability of either (L, L)

or (R, R) must also be zero. This observation helps to highlight hidden assumptions of the model. When using the mixed strategy, the decision maker does "remember" the outcome of the random factor, which determines whether he is playing "twice L" or "twice R." On the other hand, if at d_1 he employs a behavioral strategy in which he chooses L or R with some probabilities, he is not able to recall the outcome of his randomization at d_1 once he reaches d_2. This fact reflects a more general point: The model does not allow us to refer to restrictions on the memory of the strategy.

4.6 The Multiselves Approaches

Is a decision maker at one history able to control his actions at another history? In our discussion of time consistency, we assumed that when a decision maker reassesses his behavior at any particular information set, he may consider changing his planned actions at other information sets as well. This approach is in contrast with an alternative first suggested by Strotz (1956) as a framework for analyzing dynamic inconsistencies. In this alternative view, the decision maker at one information set is unable to control his behavior at future information sets. A decision maker is a collection of hypothetical agents (selves) whose plans form an equilibrium in the decision maker's own mind. Formally, for any decision problem Γ, define $G(\Gamma)$ to be the extensive game in which each information set of Γ is assigned a distinct player, and all players have the same payoffs the decision maker has. The behavior of the decision maker in Γ is then analyzed as an equilibrium of $G(\Gamma)$.

If the decision problem is one with perfect information, the game $G(\Gamma)$ has a subgame perfect equilibrium. It is well known that any optimal play for Γ is the play induced by some subgame perfect equilibrium of $G(\Gamma)$, and any subgame perfect equilibrium of $G(\Gamma)$ corresponds to an optimal strategy. This is a consequence of what in game-theoretic jargon is called the "one-deviation property."

An analogous result holds for decision problems with perfect recall and imperfect information. In this case, we use the solution concept of sequential equilibrium, which combines sequential rationality with the requirement of consistent beliefs. The set of distributions over the terminal nodes generated by the sequential equilibria of $G(\Gamma)$ is identical to the set of distributions generated by the optimal strategies of Γ (see Hendon, Jacobsen, and Sloth [1996]).

The equivalence of the single-self and the multiselves approaches for decision problems with perfect recall breaks down when we analyze decision problems with imperfect recall. Consider Example 2. The multiselves approach does not rule out the inferior strategy (L, L): conditional upon being at d_1, the choice of L is optimal if the decision maker treats his behavior at d_2 as unchangeable and believes that at d_2 he will play L. Nevertheless, the optimal strategy (R, R) is an equilibrium of the multi-selves game as well.

When coming to decision problems with absent-mindedness, the situation seems to be more complicated. It seems that for such problems we have to reconsider the definition of the multiselves approach. If each information set is modeled as one player, we implicitly assume that a "player" who is able to change his action in an information set is also able to control his behavior during other visits to this information set. If we postulate that a decision maker at each instance can control his behavior only at that instance, we are led to an alternative definition. We say that a strategy b is *modified multiselves-consistent* if for any information set X, changing the action assigned by b to the information set X is not profitable, when the decision maker assumes that in all other information sets or in any other visits to the information set X, he will continue to follow b.

Formally, b is modified multiselves-consistent if there exists a belief μ, consistent with b, such that for every information set X

reached with positive probability and for every action $a \in A(X)$ for which $b(h)(a) > 0$ for $h \in X$, there is no $a' \in A(X)$ such that

$$\Sigma_{h \in X} \mu(h) \Sigma_{z \in Z} p(z \mid (h, a'), b) u(z) > \Sigma_{h \in X} \mu(h) \Sigma_{z \in Z} p(z \mid (h, a), b) u(z).$$

Consider once again the absent-minded driver's problem. The optimal strategy is to continue with probability 2/3. The consistent beliefs assign a probability of 0.6 to the first intersection. If the decision maker anticipates that his "twin-self," if it exists, will use $p = 2/3$, then it is optimal for him to use $p = 2/3$ (or any other behavioral strategy) because he is indifferent between exiting (yielding the expected payoff 0.6[0] + 0.4[4] = 1.6) and continuing (yielding an expected payoff of 0.6[(1/3)4 + (2/3)1] + 0.4[1] = 1.6). Actually, the following is true for every decision problem:

Proposition 4.4 If a behavioral strategy is optimal, then it is modified multiselves-consistent.

Comment Some claim that Proposition 4.4 "solves" the paradoxical aspects of the absent-minded driver's example. I doubt it, because this "resolution" is based on a particular assumption about the decision maker's control of his future behavior that cannot be justified by principles of rationality. There are many situations in which a player is able to determine his actions in future instances. If we adopt the assumption that a decision maker at one point of time cannot control his behavior at any other point of time, we then find ourselves in the ridiculous situation presented in Example 2, in which nothing distinguishes between the strategy (L, L) and the superior strategy (R, R). Under circumstances in which a decision maker cannot indeed control his behavior beyond the instance in which he operates, the situation is reduced to a multiplayer game. But, I do not see why we should always make such an assumption. Moreover, in general terms, it seems important to keep the definition of a single player to be an entity that considers its present and future actions to be under its control at any one time but assumes that it does not affect the actions taken by *other* players.

4.7 On the Problematics of Using the Model

In the previous three sections, we pointed out three elements missing from the model that were immaterial regarding decision problems with perfect recall but that may be crucial to the analysis of a problem with imperfect recall. This leads us to question the appropriateness of the extensive decision problem model for analyzing imperfect recall.

Another major problem to be raised is the question of the memory of a strategy. When discussing time consistency, we assume that the decision maker's beliefs are consistent with the strategy, and when we talk about deviation from a strategy, we assume that the decision maker remembers the change he makes. The model is "silent" about the question whether the decision maker can remember the strategy he has chosen and whether he is able to recall a change in strategy if he makes one.

There are other aspects of decision making in which the model is narrow. For example, sometimes a decision maker knows that he may one day doubt the information he possesses. This fear of becoming confused is an important element in daily life and often motivates decision makers to prefer modes of behavior that keep things simple as a means to avoid the harm resulting from confusion.

Modeling confusion within an extensive decision problem is problematic. Consider the following variant of the absent-minded driver's problem (fig. 4.4): A driver is at point A and wishes to reach point C. He could drive to C via the long route, which would bring him to his destination directly without having to make any further decisions, or he could use a short but unmarked road, in which case he would have to make a turn at the second intersection. If he arrives at point B or if he misses the second intersection and reaches point D, he will be stuck in traffic and hence waste several hours in returning to C.

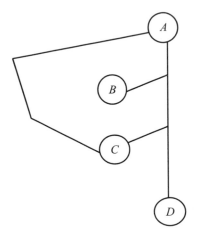

Figure 4.4

The driver knows that he is able to identify the exit to B (hereinafter #1) but that when he arrives at the exit to C (hereinafter #2),
he will become confused and believe that there is a probability of
0.1 that he has not yet passed the first intersection. The driver
believes that once he finds himself in this state of doubt, he will
become alert and no longer confused. The driver does not conclude
from his state of doubt (which would occur only at the second
intersection) that he is actually at the second intersection.

Note the difference between this problem and the absent-minded
driver's problem. In the latter, the decision maker does not distinguish between the two intersections. Here he does recognize the
first intersection but is confused when he arrives at the second.

To model the situation as an extensive decision problem, we may
depart from the assumption that the informational structure is
partitional. The player's beliefs are consistent with an information
structure, $P(\#1) = \{\#1\}$, $P(\#2) = \{\#1, \#2\}$, defined on the probability space $\Omega = \{\#1, \#2\}$ with $\pi(\#1) = 0.1$ and $\pi(\#2) = 0.9$. However,
note that game theory is not developed for games with such nonpartitional information structures (for an exception see Geanakoplos (1990)).

Recall that usually we take the extensive decision problem (or extensive game) to represent the physical order of events. If we allow the extensive problem to be a description of the decision maker's process of reasoning, then the following problem (fig. 4.5) seems to capture the decision maker's considerations:

Note that any presentation of the situation as a decision problem has to include a node, v_1, in which the choice between the short and long routes is made; a node, v_2, that corresponds to the decision problem at the turn to B; and an information set that corresponds to the state of doubt. The two nodes in this information set, v_3 and v_4, must be different from v_2 because at v_2 the decision maker does not have any doubts about his location. A chance player, which precedes this information set, enables us to model the assumption that the decision maker believes with probability 0.9 that he is at the turn to C (and will not have any further decisions to make) and with probability 0.1 that he is at the turn to B (and he will have one more decision to make at the turn to C if he continues). When

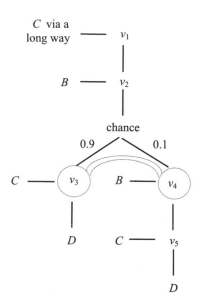

Figure 4.5

considering his action at this information set, the decision maker realizes that he may pass through the intersection to C later on as well; thus, the tree must include another successor node, v_5. Notice that by introducing this modeling device we loosen the interpretation of a history from a "possible sequences of actions." In addition, in such a case a strategy cannot be interpreted as a plan of action. Looking at the map (fig. 4.4), we observe that the decision maker could make at most three decisions (at A, at the turn to B, and at the turn to C) on one excursion. In the above problem, there is a path (v_1, v_2, v_4, v_5) in which the driver has to make four decisions. Thus, in practice, the node v_5 is unreachable. The decision at v_5 is not part of the plan of action made at A. It is added to the problem merely to allow us to discuss the decision maker's reasoning when in a state of doubt.

Thus, although this decision problem involving "confusion" can be modeled using the tools of an extensive decision problem, I am confused about the extent of its effectivity.

4.8 Bibliographic Notes

Most of the material in this chapter is based on Piccione and Rubinstein (1995). Section 7 is based on Rubinstein (1991).

The pioneering distinction between perfect and imperfect recall as well as the formalization of extensive games is due to Kuhn (1953).

The presentation of the notion of an "extensive problem" in this lecture follows the presentation of the material in Chapter 6 of Osborne and Rubinstein (1994).

4.9 Projects

1. *Exercise* Discuss the absent-minded driver's problem with the additional information that the driver is hired by an employer who, prior to the trip, gives the driver instructions as to how to behave along the highway. The driver is unable to

distinguish between the two intersections. The employer, after giving the instructions, will fall asleep and with probability $\varepsilon > 0$ may awaken at each of the intersections without knowing where he is, but he will be capable of changing his initial instructions. If he is awakened once he will not be awakened again.

2. *Exercise* Assume that the driver in Example 3, before starting his drive, can choose a "strategy" according to which he will initially follow the strategy of "exiting with probability α," but once reaching an intersection, with probability ζ, he will change his strategy to "exit with probability β." If such a "strategy" is optimal among its class, does $\alpha = \beta$?

3. *Innovative* Formulate and analyze situations such as the following: A decision maker has to choose, at two points of time, an action from a given set of alternatives with the aim of choosing the same action twice. There is a *possibility* that when he makes the second choice, he will get confused and will become uncertain about his choice in the first stage.

4. *Reading* Consider a decision problem with perfect information. The reduced decision problem is the choice from among a set of lotteries that can be obtained by employing a pure strategy. Discuss and criticize the axiomatization of Thompson (1952) for the equivalence of a decision problem to its reduced decision problem in light of the "bounded rationality" perspective. (For a presentation of Thompson's axiomatization, see Osborne and Rubinstein (1994), section 11.2.)

5. *Innovative* (Based on Rubinstein (1990).) Discuss the following two-person two-stage scenario:

Stage 1 Player 1 has to announce a string of 15 digits (0's and 1's).

Stage 2 Player 2 has to announce a string of 15 digits.

Player 2 wins if he exactly repeats the string of digits announced by player 1. If he fails, player 1 wins.

What is the conventional game theoretical treatment of the scenario? If asked, would you prefer to have the role of player 1 or of player 2? Suggest a way to model the situation to capture your answer.

5   Choosing What to Know

5.1 Optimal Information Structures

There could be numerous causes for the existence of constraints or
costs on the information held by a decision maker: the *acquisition*
of information is not a free operation; the information acquired
often has to be stored in *memory* before use, and memory is not
unbounded; and, further, when the decision maker consists of a
collection of agents, information is received through a process of
communication that has its own limits. The existence of constraints
raises the issue of deciding "what to know." In this chapter, we
analyze the problem of choosing the best information structure,
given the constraints.

A formal model that can be used to analyze the problem of the
optimal choice of information structure includes:

- a set of actions, A
- a set of states, Ω
- a probability measure π on Ω and
- a utility function, u defined on $A \times \Omega$.

An information function, P, will complete (A, Ω, u, π) to a decision
problem. If the decision maker chooses the information function P
and the state ω occurs, then the decision maker is informed "$P(\omega)$"

and chooses an action, $a(P, \omega)$, that maximizes expected utility, given the probability π conditional on the event $P(\omega)$. The value of the information partition P is thus $\text{Ex}[u(a(P, \omega), \omega)]$. A constraint on the feasible information structures is modeled by specifying a set of information structures S. We are interested in the problem $\max_{P \in S} \text{Ex}[u(a(P, \omega), \omega)]$.

In the rest of this chapter, we limit ourselves to partitional information structures. A set of information structures S will reflect constraints on the information structures originating from a given bound on the set of partitions that the decision maker can use. We will not discuss the potential tradeoff between obtaining better payoffs and expanding the set of feasible information structures.

Two economic examples are analyzed in this chapter. The selection of the economic issues as well as the "bounded rationality" elements introduced in the two examples are, admittedly, arbitrary and meant only to allow us to clarify the logic of the problem. In both examples, the decision maker does not have full information on the existing price. The reader may wonder why there should be any difficulty in fully recognizing a price; after all, a price is only a number. However, recall that it is rare for a price of a product to comprise just one number. Often, a price entails a long list of figures corresponding to features such as service fees, payment arrangements, and the length of the warranty. The multiplicity of such details makes the calculation of the "price figure" a nontrivial task. Furthermore, recognizing a price involves more than simply perceiving the posted price. In our examples, the price may depend on the state of nature and the decision maker may be interested in making inferences from the price about the prevailing state of nature. This is an even less trivial operation.

The analysis in this chapter may be relevant to the discussion of "models of rational expectations," in which economic agents deduce valuable information from the realized equilibrium prices. A common criticism of these models attacks their assumption about the economic agents' unlimited ability to deduce information from actual prices. This is actually a complex operation requiring both skill and comprehensive knowledge of the model. Because the reasoning process is not spelled out in rational expectations models, the differing abilities of economic agents in deducing information from prices do not enter into the conventional analysis. Embedding "bounded rationality" elements into a rich "rational expectations" model is certainly a serious challenge that this chapter does not even begin to address.

5.2 What Is "High" and What Is "Low"?

We often summarize our impression of a good in a store by statements such as "the price there is high" or "the price there is low." Why do we not use other terms for summarizing our experience (e.g., "the price is extreme" or "the price is a prime number")? Moreover, what determines whether a certain price is perceived as "high" or "low"? We will deal with these questions within the very narrow context of a buyer who has to buy a good in one of two stores. However, our discussion is part of an ambitious research program that proposes to explain, by the use of "economic-like" considerations, the classification systems employed for other types of objects (such as why the class of "furniture" is divided into the set "chairs" and the set "tables" and not into two other sets, "chables" and "tairs," each of which contains some chairs and some tables.)

By the approach used here, the contents of the terms "high price" and "low price" are designed to enable the decision maker to act optimally, given existing constraints on the information he can perceive or the information he can transfer from the moment he has access to information about the price in one store to the instant in which he has to take an action. This must sound too abstract, so let us move to a discussion of the following simple scenario.

A decision maker must buy one unit of an indivisible good in one of two stores. The decision maker approaches the two stores sequentially. He believes that the prices offered in the two stores, ω_1 and ω_2, are drawn from two independent (not necessarily identical) distributions, π_1 and π_2 accordingly. Let Ω_i be the (finite) set of all possible prices that may be offered in store i.

The decision maker who uses an information structure (Ω_1, P_1) for observing the first price will go through the following four stages:

Stage 1 He observes the first price $\omega_1 \in \Omega_1$.

Stage 2 He classifies ω_1 into cell $P_1(\omega_1)$. He carries with him only the name (and the meaning) of the set, $P_1(\omega_1)$, to the next stage.

Stage 3 He observes the second price $\omega_2 \in \Omega_2$.

Stage 4 He makes a decision on the basis of what he remembers about ω_1 (the cell $P_1(\omega_1)$) and the price ω_2; he buys the good from store 2 if and only if ω_2 is lower than the expected price of ω_1 conditional on being in $P_1(\omega_1)$.

We assume one nondegeneracy assumption that guarantees that the decision maker may be interested in carrying the information from the first store to the second; that is, there are ω_1^H, $\omega_1^L \in \Omega_1$ and $\omega_2 \in \Omega_2$ so that $\omega_1^H > \omega_2 > \omega_1^L$.

The problem we focus on is the rational choice of P_1, the partitional information structure of Ω_1. We impose a constraint on the choice of P_1: the number of cells in the partition it induces on Ω_1 is two. (The number two is taken here only for the sake of simplicity; the extension of the example to an arbitrary number of cells is simple.) The names of the cells in the partition are taken to be H and L. With no loss of generality, we assume that $E_H = \text{Ex}(\omega_1 \in H) \geq \text{Ex}(\omega_1 \in L) = E_L$. No constraints are imposed on the sets H and L.

To embed the problem in the more general framework described in the previous section, let $\Omega = \Omega_1 \times \Omega_2$ and $\pi(\omega) = \pi_1(\omega_1)\pi_2(\omega_2)$. The set of information structures, S, comprises those induced from a partition of Ω, of the type $\cup_{\omega_2 \in \Omega_2} \{I_1 \times \{\omega_2\}, I_2 \times \{\omega_2\}\}$, where $\{I_1, I_2\}$ is a partition of Ω_1. Thus, an information structure P satisfies $P(\omega_1, \omega_2) = P_1(\omega_1) \times \{\omega_2\}$. An action is the name of the store in which the item is bought, that is, $A = \{1, 2\}$. The payoff function is $u(a, \omega) = -\omega_a$. Given the choice of the information structure P, the chosen action $a(P, \omega)$ is 1 if $\mathrm{Ex}(\omega_1 \mid P_1(\omega)) \leq \omega_2$ and 2 otherwise.

Figure 5.1 illustrates the choice at the second stage. Note, however, that we did not assume that the entire set H is to the right of the set L (as exhibited in the diagram).

Remarks The following are three interpretations of the model which correspond to the three potential sources, delineated in Section 1, for the existence of constraints on the decision maker's information structure:

1. *Memory constraints* One can think about the model as a model of search for the lowest price, in which the decision maker faces memory constraints. After observing the price ω_1, he can remember

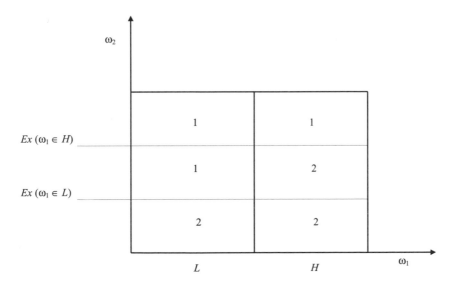

Figure 5.1

only whether the price belongs to a certain category or not. Note, however, that the term "search" is usually associated with a situation in which the decision maker is allowed to decide when to stop the search. In contrast, in this model, the decision maker cannot stop the search at the first store even if he believes he has obtained the lowest possible price.

2. *Communication constraints* Think about the decision maker as a team consisting of two agents. Agent 1 observes the price in the first store and sends a message to agent 2, who has the power to make decisions after he observes the second price. With this interpretation, the information constraints reflect the constraints on the set of messages (words) that can be sent from one individual to another.

3. *Information acquisition constraints* (suggested to me by Kathy Graddy) A decision maker must purchase one unit of a good that is sold in the market on two successive dates. At date 1, he obtains the market price of date 1, and acquires additional information about the anticipated price at date 2. On the basis of this information, he has to decide whether to buy the good at the first or at the second date (if he does not buy the good at date 1 he must buy the good at date 2). The constraints on the information about the future price reflect the decision maker's difficulties in analyzing the market. Here, the decision maker can receive an answer, true or false, to only one question of the type "Will the price at the second date be in the set X?" The decision maker's problem is to choose the set X. To fit this scenario into the model, identify the price in date 1 with ω_2, and the price in date 2 with ω_1!

We now turn to the analysis of the model. What can be said about the optimal partition of Ω_1? The following result "justifies" the use of the names "high price" and "low price" for the two sets.

Proposition 5.1 Let $\{H, L\}$ be an optimal partition of Ω_1. Any price $\omega_1 > \lambda^* = \mathrm{Ex}\{\omega_2 \mid E_L < \omega_2 \leq E_H\}$ is in H and any price $\omega_1 < \lambda^*$ is in L.

Proof First, note that if $\{H, L\}$ is an optimal partition of Ω_1, then there is a price $\omega_2 \in \Omega_2$ in the interval $(E_L, E_H]$. If there is no such ω_2, then the optimal decision is independent of the information obtained about ω_1. This cannot be an optimal behavior because of the nondegeneracy assumption (given the existence of $\omega_1^H, \omega_1^L \in \Omega_1$ and $\omega_2 \in \Omega_2$ so that $\omega_1^H > \omega_2 > \omega_1^L$, it would be better for the decision maker to put one of the two prices, ω_1^H or ω_1^L, into one cell and all the rest in the other).

Assume now that there is $\lambda \in \Omega_1$ so that $\lambda < \lambda^*$ and $\lambda \in H$. Transfer λ to the set L. Even if the action decision is not updated (that is, the decision maker continues to choose store 2 if and only if $\omega_1 \in H$ and $\omega_2 < E_H$ or $\omega_1 \in L$ and $\omega_2 < E_L$), the transition by itself reduces the expected price (and may reduce it even further if the decision at the second store adjusts to the change in the content of the partition of Ω_1). This is because the only change in the action taken occurs when $\omega_1 = \lambda$ and $E_L \leq \omega_2 < E_H$. The decision maker formerly chose store 2 and now chooses store 1, and by the assumption that $\lambda < \mathrm{Ex}\{\omega_2 \mid E_L < \omega_2 \leq E_H\}$, the change reduces his expected payment. An analogous argument applies to $\lambda > \lambda^*$. $\square$

The proposition shows that the optimal way to partition the prices in the first store is into two categories, "high" and "low," where a "high" price means that it is above some cutoff point and a "low" price means that it is below that cutoff point. The proposition also provides a qualitative characterization of the cutoff point in terms of the price distributions. At the optimal partition, the cutoff point has to be the expectation of ω_2 conditional on the interval $(E_L, E_H]$.

5.3 Manipulating Informational Restrictions

In almost all models in economic theory, behavioral differences among agents are attributed to differences in preferences or in the information they possess. But there are economic phenomena better attributed not to these factors but to differences in the ability to process information. Rarely do two readers of the same morning newspaper, who wish to make money in Wall Street, interpret what they read identically and then make the same decisions.

In this section, like the previous one, each economic agent has to choose an information structure, subject to the constraints that express his ability to process information, and in response to the environment in which he operates. Economic agents will differ in their constraints imposed on the information structures they can use. Other, quite sophisticated economic agents will take advantage of the differences.

We start from the following simple model of a market with a single good produced by a single seller, and two buyers, each of whom is interested in consuming only one unit of the commodity (fig. 5.2). The economic parameters of the market depend on the state of nature, which may be either ω_H or ω_L. All agents share the initial belief that the two states are equally likely. Production ensues after an order is received. In state ω_L, the seller's production costs, c_L, are constant zero. In state ω_H, the seller's production costs depend on the identity of the consumers who purchase the commodity (this assumption fits a service good in particular). Let c_i be the cost of producing a unit for consumer i in state ω_H. A consumer purchases the good if and only if the expected surplus is strictly positive, where the surplus derived from consuming one unit of the commodity at state s for the price p is $v_s - p$. We restrict the values and the costs so that $c_1 > v_H > c_2 > v_L > 0$.

The basic seller's dilemma is that at state ω_H, he cannot gain from selling the good to consumer 1 inasmuch as the cost of producing that good is higher than the maximum price consumer 1 is ready to pay. Therefore, at state ω_H, the seller would like to sell the good only to consumer 2. However, the price mechanism does not enable the seller to discriminate between agents. A unique price must prevail in each instance. It is assumed further that conditional on state ω_H, the seller prefers not to sell any amount over selling two

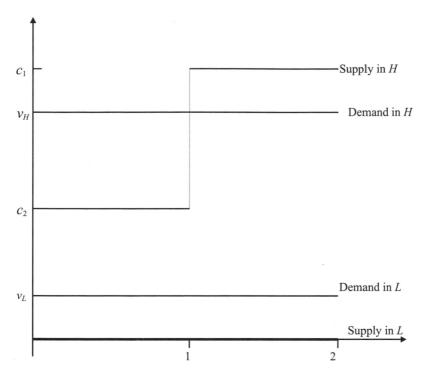

c_1 — Supply in H

v_H — Demand in H

c_2

v_L — Demand in L

Supply in L

1   2

Figure 5.2

units even for the maximum price of v_H, that is, $2v_H < c_2 + c_1$. The order of events in the market is assumed to be as follows:

Stage 1 The seller announces a price policy that is a specification of a "lottery" of prices (a probability measure with finite support) for each of the states of nature. The seller's announcement is a *commitment* to supply the good, if demanded by any of the consumers at the price resulting from the lottery following the realization of the state of nature.

Stage 2 Nature selects the state of nature and the seller's offer is determined by the probabilistic device to which the seller has committed himself.

Stage 3 The consumers are informed about the realization of the lottery. On the basis of the posted price and the announced price policy, each consumer has to make a decision whether to accept or reject the offer.

Up to now, the model is a conventional leader-followers (Stackelberg) situation, in which the seller is the leader who chooses the price policy and the two consumers are the followers who choose the acceptance rules. It can easily be verified that the seller's upper bound on his expected profits is v_L. To see that he can (almost) achieve this level of profits, notice that by charging $v_L - \varepsilon$ in state ω_L and charging a price above v_H in state ω_H, the seller's expected profits are close to v_L (we forgo the details of the uninteresting proof that the seller cannot indeed achieve profits above v_L by any price strategy, even if he employs random devices).

Remarks

1. The seller's strategy is the choice of a random device for every state of nature. In reality, such a seller's strategy can be obtained, for example, through contracting with a retailer in a manner dependent on random elements. Although he employs random devices, the seller's strategy is a *pure* strategy, not a mixed strategy. The strategy determines the consumers' beliefs and behavior, and therefore the seller may strictly prefer a strategy with stochastic elements over any strategy that specifies a deterministic price for each state.

2. Given the consumers' purchasing strategies, the seller may be better off by not following the announced price policy after the state of nature is realized. But the seller is committed to the policy he has announced and the posted price *must* be determined according to the random device that the announced strategy has assigned to the realized state of nature.

3. This construction avoids the need to discuss "out-of-equilibrium" prices. Because the price policy is a commitment, only prices in the support of the equilibrium price policy can be materialized. The seller's announcement forces all fully rational consumers to

hold the same beliefs abut the state of nature after the realization of the price.

We are ready to add the "bounded rationality" feature to the basic economic model—the imperfection in the consumer's ability to recognize the price. A decision maker has to choose "what to know" about the price. Given the information he will receive, he will have to take an action ("buy" or "don't buy"). We constrain the information structures available to the consumer to those in which the partition of the potential prices consists of connected intervals. An agent's ability is modeled by the number of sets in the partition (that is, the number of cutoff points plus 1).

Assume that consumer 1 is able to determine only *one* cutoff point, that is, he can split the price space into only two connected sets, whereas consumer 2 is able to determine *two* cutoff points, which split the price space into three connected sets. The assumption that the cost of production for consumer 1 (the less able consumer) is higher than for consumer 2 (the more able consumer) especially fits for commodities like education and consulting services. The selection of the partition is carried out by each of the consumers between stages 1 and 2, that is, after the buyers learn the announced price *policy* and before the realization of the price. The decision concerning the partition is subject to the personal restrictions imposed. The order of events in the modified model is as follows:

Stage 1 The seller announces a price policy.

Stage 1.5 Each consumer selects a partition (given the constraints determined by the consumer's abilities).

Stage 2 Nature selects the state and the price is determined.

Stage 3 Each consumer is informed of the cell in his partition that includes the announced price and decides whether to purchase the good.

Discussion

In terms of the general framework described in the first section, the state space Ω consists of all pairs (s, p), where p is a price that may be offered in state $s \in \{\omega_H, \omega_L\}$. The seller's price policy determines the probability distribution over Ω. A partition on the price space induces a partition of Ω.

The restriction on the information partitions can be thought of as a bound on the complexity of the consumer's acceptance strategy. Consumer 1 has only two categories of prices, "high" and "low," and his decision whether or not to accept the offer depends on the price being in one of these categories. Consumer 2 can classify prices into three categories—"high," "medium," and "low"—and thus can also adopt an acceptance rule of the type "buy if the price is medium and don't buy otherwise." The designation of a price as "high," "medium," or "low" is chosen by the consumer.

Note that we assume that the decision maker has a restricted ability to "know" or to "recognize" the price, but, at the same time, is able to make complicated calculations in order to determine the optimal partition. Actually, the contrast in the model between the decision maker's constraints on knowledge and, concurrently, his unlimited ability to optimize is a "tension" prevailing in many models of bounded rationality. One may wonder about this assumption. Allowing full rationality on one level and partial rationality on another level is, in my opinion, a sound assumption for modeling situations in which the decision maker faces a routine decision problem and, from time to time, gives thought to the rule of behavior he uses regularly while taking into account the constraints he faces regarding the rules he can implement.

Analysis

We now come to the main point of this section. It will be shown that the seller can utilize the differences between consumers to obtain profits arbitrarily close to his ideal profit level, $\Pi^* = v_L + (v_H - c_2)/2$. The idea is quite simple: Choose "small" positive numbers ε_L and ε_H so that $\varepsilon_L > \varepsilon_H$ and choose the probability number π slightly above max $\{2\varepsilon_H/(v_H - v_L), \varepsilon_L/[\varepsilon_L + (v_H - v_L)/2]\}$. Note that π can be chosen to be arbitrarily small.

Consider the following price strategy:

- In state ω_H, charge the price $v_H - \varepsilon_H$ with probability 1;
- In state ω_L, charge the price $(v_H + v_L)/2$ with probability π and $v_L - \varepsilon_L$ with probability $1 - \pi$.

Given this strategy, the price space is $\{v_L - \varepsilon_L, (v_H + v_L)/2, v_H - \varepsilon_H\}$. The price $(v_H + v_L)/2$ is a "mine" put by the seller. A buyer who buys the good at this price suffers a "big" loss because it is offered only in state ω_L, where the value of the good is v_L. The appearance of the other two prices are correlated with the state so that a purchase yields a positive surplus.

Consumer 2 is able to partition the price space into three sets and to purchase the good only at the profitable high and low prices. Conversely, consumer 1 can place only one cutoff point. We distinguish between two cases.

Case i Consumer 1 places the cutoff point between $v_L - \varepsilon_L$ and $(v_H + v_L)/2$. Hence, if the price falls in the low category, he infers that the state is ω_L, the price is $v_L - \varepsilon_L$, and he buys the good. If the price falls in the high category, he cannot infer whether the state is ω_H (and the deal is profitable) or the state is ω_L (and the deal is disastrous); having $\pi > 2\varepsilon_H/(v_H - v_L)$ makes consumer 1 prefer to reject the offer.

Case ii Consumer 1 chooses a cutoff point between $(v_H + v_L)/2$ and $v_H - \varepsilon_H$. He then buys the good if the price is high and does not if the price is low, because $\pi > 2\varepsilon_H/[\varepsilon_L + (v_H - v_L)/2]$.

Thus, for consumer 1, the choice of a cutoff point amounts to the choice between either purchasing the good at ω_L for the price $v_L - \varepsilon_L$ with probability $(1 - \pi)/2$ or at ω_H for the price $v_H - \varepsilon_H$ with probability $1/2$. One can choose π, ε_H and ε_L so that the former is better for consumer 1, so both consumers buy in state ω_L and only consumer 2 buys in state ω_H, and the seller's profits are arbitrarily close to Π^*.

5.4 Perceptrons

It has already been mentioned that one of the origins of the difficulties in processing information about a price is that in real life, a price is often a vector of components. In this section, we continue to use the basic economic model described in the previous section, but with one major change: It is assumed explicitly that the seller splits the price of the commodity into K components. A realized offer is a K-tuple $(p_1, \ldots, p_K)$. A consumer who accepts the seller's offer $(p_1, \ldots, p_K)$ pays Σp_k. The manner in which the sum Σp_k is divided among the K components may contain relevant information concerning market conditions. Agents may experience difficulty in decoding that information from the vector and they may differ in their ability to do so.

The consumers in the current model will employ a certain type of machine to make their calculation. The computing machine is called a *perceptron*. Its characteristics are a threshold number, α^*, and a set of *sensors*, $\phi_1, \ldots, \phi_M$. In the first stage of the perceptron's operation, the sensors operate in parallel on the realized price vector. Each ϕ_m is a function that operates on some of the components of the price vector, receives the values of those components as input, and provides a real number as an output. In the second stage, the sum of the sensors' outputs, $\Sigma_m \phi_m$, is calculated in the "center" and its value is compared with α^*.

Figure 5.3 is a schematic illustration of a perceptron.

Of course, no claim is made that this computational device is part of the "true" description of the human processing of a vector of price components.

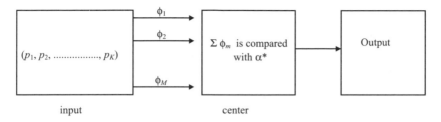

Figure 5.3

We are now ready to insert the imperfection in the consumers' calculations into the model. Consumers are bounded in the complexity of the perceptrons they can use. The complexity of a perceptron, its order, is taken as the number of components in the domain of its sensors. If each ϕ_m depends on only one of the p_k's, then ϕ is a perceptron of *order 1*; if each ϕ_m is a function of two prices, the perceptron is of *order 2*. Consumers have no restrictions on the number of sensors, and they have perfect ability to calculate the sum and to compare it with the threshold level, α^*. The final action (to accept or reject the offer) may depend on only this comparison. Thus, the complexity of a perceptron reflects the complexity of the sensor, the unit that executes the basic calculation performed by the perceptron, and the complexity of the sensor is measured by the number of variables involved in the calculation. (This is somewhat similar to the comparison between personal computers on the basis of the complexity of the basic processor.)

Consumers differ with respect to the orders of the perceptrons they are able to employ. Consumer 2 is able to employ perceptrons of order 2 whereas consumer 1 is constrained to use only perceptrons of order 1.

To summarize the structure of the model, as in the previous section the seller first announces a price policy that assigns a lottery of *price vectors* to every state. The seller is committed to that policy. Next, every consumer has to choose a perceptron (constrained by the order he can use). Finally, the price vector is realized and each consumer decides, on the basis of the information computed by his perceptron, whether to purchase the commodity or not.

In the following, we will see that in this model as in the previous section, the seller can approach his maximal expected profits level, Π^*. Consider the following price strategy: The seller splits the price of the commodity into two components. Let $a = v_H/2 - \varepsilon_H$ and $b = v_L/2 - \varepsilon_L$. In state ω_H, the seller chooses the vector (a, a) with probability 1. In state ω_L, he chooses the vector (b, b) with probability $1 - \delta$, and each of the vectors (a, b) and (b, a) with probability $\delta/2$.

Consumer 2 is able to avoid the trap of purchasing the good for the price $a + b$ at state ω_L by employing, for example, a perceptron of order 2, with one sensor, which gives the value 1 for the vectors (a, a) and (b, b), and the value -1 for the vectors (a, b) and (b, a), setting $\alpha^* = 0$. (Alternatively, since $p_1 = p_2$ iff $p_1^2 + p_2^2 - 2p_1p_2 = (p_1 - p_2)^2 \le 0$, he can use a perceptron with one sensor of order 2 and two sensors of order 1.)

Consumer 1 cannot pursue a strategy in which he buys the commodity only at the price vectors (a, a) and (b, b). If such a purchasing strategy existed, there would be *two* sensors (more than two will not help), ϕ_1 and ϕ_2, and a number α^* so that the sums $\phi_1(b) + \phi_2(b)$ and $\phi_1(a) + \phi_2(a)$ would be on one side of α^* and the sums $\phi_1(a) + \phi_2(b)$ and $\phi_1(b) + \phi_2(a)$ on the other. This is clearly impossible.

Now, we can choose arbitrarily "small" numbers, δ, ε_H and ε_L, $\varepsilon_L > \varepsilon_H$, so that consumer 1

1. would prefer to avoid purchasing the commodity with probability $\delta/4$ for the price $a + b$, even if he were to buy the commodity at state ω_H for the price $a + a$, and

2. would prefer to purchase the good for the price $b + b$ in state ω_L rather than purchasing the good for the price $a + a$ in state ω_H.

Thus, as in the previous section, the seller forces consumer 1 to focus attention on escaping the trap he has prepared for him by (sometimes) offering a high price in ω_L. Being preoccupied with this fear, consumer 1 cannot devote his limited computational resources to the task of identifying the conditions under which it is desirable for him to purchase the commodity for a high price. In contrast, consumer 2 is able to infer the true state from the seller's price strategy and is able both to escape the trap and to identify the conditions under which paying a high price is profitable.

Remark Within the context of "Industrial Organization," the model shows that the complexity of the price scheme can be used strategically by price setters. Casual observation confirms that price schedules are complex and that the complexity of the price structure affects the behavior of economic agents. The closest relevant economic literature concerns equilibrium in markets with search. In these models, a consumer makes his purchasing decision through a search process. Search in these models is not necessarily a physical activity, but can be thought of as a mental process. Consequently, the search costs can be interpreted as the costs associated with the searcher's difficulties in recognizing prices as opposed to physical sampling costs. Within the literature attempting to explain price dispersion, the closest to our approach is Salop (1977), where all consumers know the prices available in the market but do not know what store charges what price. A consumer has to choose either to purchase the good at random or to incur an exogenously given cost in obtaining the information about the location of the store charging the lowest price. The cost associated with getting the information is heterogeneously distributed among the consumers. Assuming a correlation between the consumer's search cost and other consumer characteristics, Salop (1977) shows that the model allows an optimal strategy for a monopolist where more than one price is charged.

5.5 Bibliographic Notes

Section 2 is based on Dow (1991). Sections 3 and 4 are based on Rubinstein (1993).

Related papers to Section 2 are Fershtman and Kalai (1993), Meyer (1991), Rosenthal (1993), and Yampuler (1995). For an introduction to the notion of perceptrons, see Minsky and Papert (1988).

5.6 Projects

1. *Exercise* (Based on Yampuler [1995]). An employer wishes to employ one of two agents 1 and 2. If he employs agent i, he obtains v_i, which is the realization of a random variable distributed uniformly in the interval [0, 1]. The realization of v_i is private information held by agent i. The employer can force agent i to reveal v_i, or he can leave it to the agent to decide whether to disclose v_i or not. If an agent chooses to disclose v_i, he can do it only truthfully. The constraint on the employer's ability to process information is that if both agents submit reports, he is able to "read" only one of the reports. The employer's aim is to maximize the expected value he obtains from the agent whom he employs. Each agent has lexicographic priorities: primarily to be employed, secondarily not to submit a report (there are implicit costs associated with the submission). Thus, if an agent has no chance of being employed, he would prefer not to submit the report.

Show that there is a "mechanism" (in which agents are *not required* to disclose their values, although they are permitted to do so) in which the employer's equilibrium expected profits are strictly higher than those obtained by using any mechanism that *requires* the two agents to disclose their values.

2. *Reading* Read Meyer (1991). Provide an explanation for the *advantage* often given in the second round of a two-round competition to the winner of the first round. For the explanation, construct a model in which A and B are two competitors. The true relative strength of the competitors (the state) may be either A^{++} = "A is much better," A^+ = "A is better," B^+ = "B is better," or B^{++} = "B is much better." Initially, the probability of each of the relative strengths is $1/4$. The chances of a competitor to win a match depend stochastically on the relative strength and on the type of the match. In a "fair match," the chances of A winning in state A^{++} (or A^+) is equal to the chances of B winning in state B^{++} (or B^+). Giving an advantage to competitor X is viewed as biasing the probabilities in favor of X. Assume that the design of a two-round competition is aimed to increase the probability that the better competitor will be declared the winner. Show that the optimal competition is to have a fair match at the first round followed by a match in which the winner of the first match gets an advantage.

3. *Reading* Read Fershtman and Kalai (1993) and build a game-theoretical model in which (a) a player is constrained in the complexity of the strategy he can use, in the sense that he can choose a strategy dependent on a limited number of contingencies, and (b) the more sophisticated a player, the better his equilibrium situation.

4. *Innovative* Try to find an economic model (better than the model presented in Section 3) in which the heterogeneity of agents' abilities to behave in an economic situation will play a key role in explaining some interesting economic phenomena.

5. *Exercise* In the model presented in Section 4, the seller's strategy uses four price vectors: (a, a), (b, b), (a, b), and (b, a). Investigate whether both of the two consumers can determine the realized cell of each of the following partitions:

1. $\{\{(a, a), (b, b)\}, \{(a, b), (b, a)\}\}$
2. $\{\{(a, a), (a, b), (b, a)\}, \{(b, b)\}\}$
3. $\{\{(b, b), (b, a), (a, b)\}, \{(a, a)\}\}$
4. $\{\{(a, b)\}, \{(a, a), (b, a), (b, b)\}\}$.

6. *Innovative* Construct a model in which opinions of group members are aggregated in order to determine a group decision and the aggregation is accomplished by a perceptron. Use the model to derive interesting results about aggregation rules.

7. *Reading* Read Cho (1995) and find another economic model in which the behavior of economic agents is fruitfully described by perceptrons.

6 Modeling Complexity in Group Decisions

6.1 Introduction

When we talk about a "decision maker" in economics, we often refer not to a single individual but to an entity that produces a decision in a process involving more than one individual. In this chapter we will refer to such a decision maker as an *organization*.

In most economic models, organizations that make decisions are treated as if they were rational individuals, maximizing a well-defined numerical function. In contrast, here we are interested in the way that organizations operate. In real life, organizations that make decisions are often also involved in their implementation. This activity, however, does not lie in the scope of the present discussion. Instead, we focus on activities like collecting information and computation. The discussion falls into the "bounded rationality" agenda because the design of an organization is typically motivated by concerns such as its "complexity," the cost of its operation, and the speed by which a decision is made.

We will discuss three models, each of which captures different bounds on the operation of an organization. In the first, the model of teams, each agent has to take an action based on information that he has observed or received through a costly communication channel from other members of the team. In the second model, Radner's model of organization, the group has to pursue an action based on information it gathers from many sources. In the third, that of social choice, a collective decision has to be made on the basis of information obtained about the members' preferences.

Some of the questions posed here are similar to those asked regarding individual decision makers. When discussing the team model, we will ask, "Does the decision process lead to a rational decision?" and "Does decentralization lead to centralized optimization?" When discussing an organization as a mechanism for collecting information, we will view the organization as a process of production and investigate the shape of its production function. Regarding social-choice rules, we will try to identify rules that are relatively simple.

A close connection exists between the models discussed in this chapter and the design of automatic systems as discussed in computer science. Of course, the constraints on a computer system are dictated by its special hardware limitations. Nevertheless, in both fields, the information is held initially by numerous agents and has to be collected and processed to produce the desired output. Note, however, an important difference: In automatic systems, the designer does not have to take into account the possibility that the "agents" will not obey the instructions they receive. In building human organizations, a basic concern involves the provision of the correct compliance incentives to the agents.

6.2   The Model of a Team

In this section, we will discuss briefly a simple version of one of the pioneering models of organizations, Marschak and Radner's model of a *team*. A team consists of a group of agents $N = \{1, \ldots, n\}$. Each agent i has to take an action a_i from among a given set A_i. All the agents share the same preferences. Let $u(a_1, \ldots, a_n, \omega)$, be the von Neumann-Morgenstern utility obtained from the profile of actions $(a_i)_{i \in N}$ at the state $\omega \in \Omega$. Each member i has access to a signal x_i. Ideally, if there were no constraints or costs on the information, all members would be asked to share the information they acquire. However, two types of costs are involved: costs of observation and costs of communication. These costs provide the rationale for the use of a partial communication network.

The team operates in three successive stages: At each stage, the designated actions are undertaken simultaneously:

1. *Information Acquisition* Each agent i can choose to observe his signal x_i at a cost c_i.

2. *Communication* If there is an open channel from agent i to agent j, and if i observes his signal, that signal is transferred to agent j as well. A cost $d_{i,j}$ is attached to a channel of communication from i to j. The existence of any channel of communication is independent of the value of the signals received.

3. *Actions* Each agent takes an action a_i from A_i. The sets of actions are fixed and no option is available for delegating authority to take actions to other agents.

A protocol is a specification of three items: (1) a set of agents who make observations, (2) a set of communication channels, and (3) for each agent i, instructions dictating what action to take contingent on the information he acquires or receives. The team's problem is to find the best protocol. Note the difference between the team problem and the classical implementation problem, which focuses on strategic issues.

Although highly specific, the model is quite rich and allows for a variety of protocols reminiscent of real life organizations. For example, a "routine" is a protocol where no information is acquired and no communication is transferred; a "decentralized team" is a protocol where each agent receives a signal and no channel of communication to other agents is open; an "incomplete centralized information" protocol is one where only one agent observes a signal and sends it to all other agents.

What can be accomplished by this model? Of course, one can try to characterize optimal protocols under specific assumptions. We can also ask whether the team can work without a central planner and whether the team can exhibit intransitivities. In the rest of this section, we will briefly touch on these issues.

Is Centralization Needed?

Let us take the information acquisition and the communication stages as fixed and focus on the action instructions. First, note that no agent should deviate from the instructions if they result from the team's expected utility maximization and if an agent, when evaluating the execution of the instructions given to him, maximizes his expected utility given the information he possesses and assumes that all other agents follow the instructions given to them.

Without instructions, agents' decision problems as to what actions to take form a game situation with the n agents being the players, all of whom have the same utility. Of course, a non-optimal equilibrium might exist. Consider the complete information case of a two-agent team that has to coordinate its actions. Let $A_1 = A_2 = \{a, b\}$ with the utilities $u(a, a) = 1$, $u(b, b) = 2$, and $u(a, b) = u(b, a) = 0$. Then (a, a) is a non-optimal equilibrium.

Some similarity can be found between the decentralization problem of a team and the analysis of decision problems with imperfect recall. Like the multiselves in a decision problem with imperfect recall, agents in an organization share the same payoffs but do not share the same information. Solving the team problem is, therefore, analogous to the choice of an ex-ante optimal strategy. Nevertheless, only a few decision problems with imperfect recall have counterparts to teams since in the team model, each agent moves only once and all agents move simultaneously. Thus, for example, a team cannot exhibit absent-mindedness.

A Team Decision May Look Intransitive

Team choices may exhibit intransitivity. Consider a team that has to make three choices, one from each of the sets $\{a, b\}$, $\{b, c\}$ and $\{a, c\}$. There are four equally likely states: α, β, γ, and δ. The team consists of three agents, 1, 2, and 3; each gets a signal telling him whether a certain state, α, β or γ, respectively, occurs or not. The acquisition of the signal is "cheap," but communication is "expensive." Each agent can choose an action of the type (S, x), where S is one of the three choice problems and $x \in S$. The interpretation of "agent i chooses (S, x)" is that agent i takes responsibility for the choice problem S and picks $x \in S$. Assume that the payoff to the team is the sum of the payoffs it gets from the three sets. If no i chooses (S, x) or if there are two agents i and j who choose (S, x_i) and (S, x_j) respectively, the payoff accumulated by the team from the set S is 0. If only a single agent chooses (S, x) then a payoff $u(x, \omega)$ is obtained according to the following table:

	α	β	γ	δ
a	1	2	0	0
b	0	1	2	0
c	2	0	1	0

Clearly, the best protocol calls for agent 3 to decide about $\{a, b\}$ because a should be chosen unless the state is γ and agent 3 is the only agent informed about γ. Similarly the best protocol calls for agent 1 to decide about $\{b, c\}$, and agent 2 to decide about $\{a, c\}$. However, this means that in the state of nature δ, the decisions will exhibit intransitivity: The action a is chosen from $\{a, b\}$, b from $\{b, c\}$ and c from $\{a, c\}$.

Collecting Information

Consider a team that is designed to guess the value of a variable ω_0 based on the "noisy" signals $(x_i)_{i \in \{1, 2, \ldots, n\}}$ received by the agents

(n is taken to be an odd number). The value of ω_0 is either 0 or 1, each with probability $1/2$. A state is a vector $\omega = (\omega_i)_{i=0,1,\ldots,n} \in \{0, 1\}^{\{0,1,\ldots,n\}}$, where ω_i is the value of i's signal (that is, $x_i(\omega) = \omega_i$). The probability of the state $(\omega_i)_{i=0,1,\ldots,n}$ is $1/2[p]^{\#\{i|\omega_i=\omega_0\}}[1-p]^{\#\{i|\omega_i\neq\omega_0\}}$ that is, the value of agent i's signal is ω_0, with probability p. We assume $p > 1/2$. For each i, $A_i = \{0, 1\}$ is interpreted as the set of recommendations available to agent i. The recommendation of the majority determines the team's guess. The utility $u(a_1, \ldots, a_n, \omega)$ is 1 if the team's guess is equal to ω_0 and 0 otherwise. Assume that no cost is involved in agent i's acquisition of his own signal and that communication is possible only between agent i and his "two neighbors," $i - 1(\text{mod } n)$ and $i + 1(\text{mod } n)$.

One may believe that opening the channels from agent i's neighbors to agent i cannot be harmful, because if agent i knows more, the quality of his recommendation can just be improved. This is not true. The protocol in which each agent gets to know his two neighbors' signals and recommends the majority of the three signals he is exposed to is strictly worse (at least for $n \geq 9$) than the no-communication protocol in which each agent recommends his own signal. (To see this, note for example that if $(\omega_0; \omega_1, \ldots, \omega_9) = (0; 1, 1, 0, 1, 1, 0, 0, 0, 0)$, the protocol with communication causes the wrong recommendation to be accepted.)

The Limitations of Simultaneous Communication

In the team model, the content of the message sent from i to j can be only the content of i's signal. This is not a limitation under the assumption of simultaneous communication. However, if communication could be conducted sequentially, a message from one agent to another might reflect more than the information about the agent's own signal. It could include information derived from other agents' signals as well. For example, consider a three-agent team problem where the team's decision is about "the team member who will receive one unit of an available indivisible object." Assume that agent i's value of the unit, v_i, can be either 0 or v_i^*, where $v_1^* > v_2^* > v_3^* > 0$. Agent i freely receives the information about v_i. Assume that the cost of three or more communication channels is too high to be worthwhile. As to the actions to be taken, assume that each agent can either "claim" the object or not. In the case where more than one agent claims the object, the object "disintegrates." Clearly, by using two communication channels there is no way to allocate the object with certainty to the member who values it most. But, if the agents communicate in two stages, agent 1 first sends a message about his value to agent 2, who sends a message to agent 3 about the $\max\{v_1, v_2\}$: the "first best" allocation can then be obtained.

6.3 Processing Information

In this section, we discuss a model in which an organization is viewed as a collection of computational devices that can carry out a certain type of calculation. In the model, each pair of units can be instructed to execute a simple operation (such as adding two values registered in the two units and storing the outcome in one of the units). The organization's performance will be evaluated by the size of the input it processes and the speed by which the calculation is done.

More specifically, the task of the organization is to compute a function $f(x_1, \ldots, x_n)$. The basic binary operation is $g(x, y)$. The discussion is applicable to any case in which g is commutative ($g(x, y) = g(y, x)$), and associative ($g(g(x, y), z) = g(x, g(y, z))$), and the function f can be expressed as the composition of $n - 1$ iterations of the binary operation g.

A primary example is the function $f(x_1, \ldots, x_n) = \min\{x_1, \ldots, x_n\}$ with the binary operation $g(x, y) = \min\{x, y\}$. An interpretation offered for this example is that of choosing the best (cheapest) element from a group of alternatives by a process of binary comparisons. Other examples are summing up n numbers ($f(x_1, \ldots,$ $x_n) = \Sigma_i x_i$ with $g(x, y) = x + y$), and collecting information from n sources (x_i being a set of facts, $f(x_1, \ldots, x_n) = \cup_i x_i$, and $g(x, y) = x \cup y$).

In this section, an organization is a set of registers combined with a program that determines its operation. The registers are divided into three types:

1. I, a set of *input registers,* in which the input is initially stored.

2. P, a set of *computing registers* capable of making the basic calculation.

3. O, a (unique) *output register,* which obtains the output of the calculation.

All input registers start with some values and all other registers start "empty."

A *command* $p \rightarrow q$ is a pair where $p \in I \cup P$ *and* $q \in P \cup \{O\}$. A command $p \rightarrow q$ is interpreted as an operation in which:

1. If q is "empty," "take the value from p and put it in q."

2. If q is not empty, "put $g(x, y)$ in q, where x is q's value and y is p's value."

A *program* is a list of sets of commands, ($S^1, \ldots, S^{T+1}$) (the set S^t is the set of commands executed at date t) satisfying:

1. If $p \rightarrow q$ is in S^t and $p \in P$, then there exists $t' < t$ so that $p' \rightarrow p$ is in $S^{t'}$.

2. If $p \rightarrow q$ and $p' \rightarrow q'$ are in S^t, then $\{p, q\}$ and $\{p', q'\}$ are disjoint sets.

3. S^{T+1} includes a unique command of the type $p \rightarrow O$ and is the only set that includes a command involving the output register.

By (1), a register is used only after it receives a value. By (2), any register can be involved in the execution of only one command in any unit of time. By (3), the program stops as soon as the output register gets a value.

The execution of a program, whatever the input is, must yield an output. This is so because there is at least one chain of commands, $(p_i \rightarrow p_{i+1})$, starting with an input register ending with O so that $(p_i \rightarrow p_{i+1})$ is a command in S^{t_i} with $t_i < t_{i+1}$. Thus, each program induces a function that assigns an output value to every n-tuple of input values. We say that the program *calculates the function* f if its output for any n-tuple of values $x_1, \ldots, x_n$ is $f(x_1, \ldots, x_n)$.

We evaluate a program by n, the size of I, and the length of the calculation, T.

Comments Notice two of the implicit assumptions of the definition of a program. First, there is only one output outlet. In many real-life organizations, an output can be produced by several units (for example, each agent can call the fire department without having to go through the whole internal hierarchy). Second, each command is independent of the values stored in the registers. In contrast, one can imagine an organization that collects information in which the "address" for the content in p depends on the content itself.

Proposition Let m be the number of registers in P and assume that $m < n$. Then, the minimal delay for calculating f is $[n/m]_- + [\log_2(m + n(\text{mod } m))]_+$, where $[x]_-$ is the maximal integer $\leq x$ and $[x]_+$ is the minimal integer $\geq x$.

Proof For a program to execute the calculation of $f(x_1, \ldots, x_n)$ it must be that for every $p \in I$, there is a chain of commands $\{p_i \rightarrow p_{i+1}\}_{i=0,\ldots,K}$ with $p_0 = p$ and $p_{K+1} = O$ where $p_i \rightarrow p_{i+1}$ is in S^{t_i} with $t_i < t_{i+1}$.

Consider a program that calculates the function $f(x_1, \ldots, x_n)$ with minimal delay using m computing registers. We will show that such a program exists and satisfies the following properties:

1. For any $p \in I$, there is a unique q so that $p \to q$ is a command. Start with a minimal delay program that calculates f: for each $p \in I$, eliminate from the program all commands $p \to x$ excluding one which is part of a chain from p to O. Then, eliminate successively all commands that cannot be executed (any $x \to y$ in S^t so that x is empty at the tth stage). We are left with a program that computes the function f satisfying property (1).

2. For any $p \in P$ for which there is a command $q \to p$, there is a unique p' so that $p \to p'$ is in the program.

The proof is similar to that which guarantees a minimal delay program satisfying (1).

We say that p is unemptied at date t^* if the latest command prior to t^* involving p is of the form $p' \to p$. The register p is idle at t if there is no command in S^t that involves p.

3. There is no period t, command $p \to q$ in S^t with $p, q \in P$, and input register x which is unemptied at t.

If so, we can add $x \to q$ to the set S^t, eliminate $p \to q$, and replace $x \to y$ in $S^{t'}$ ($t' > t$) with $p \to y$.

4. At no period t are there two idle unemptied registers, p and q.

If there are two unemptied registers, p and q, that are idle at period t, we can add the command $p \to q$ to S^t and delete the command $p \to y$ in $S^{t'}$ ($t' > t$).

These four steps guarantee that there is a minimal delay program in which at the first $t = [n/m]_-$ steps, $n - n(\text{mod } m)$ input registers are emptied into the m computing registers. After this first phase, we are left with $n_t = m + n(\text{mod } m)$ unemptied registers, and $[n_t/2]_-$ commands can be executed, leaving us, at the beginning of date $t + 1$, with $n_{t+1} = [n_t/2]_+$ unemptied registers, and so on. After an additional $[\log_2(m + n(\text{mod } m))]_+$ stages, we are left with one register that is emptied into O. $\square$

Note that the expression $[n/m]_- + [\log_2(m + n(\text{mod } m))]_+$ is a concave function of n (modulo the integer problem). This means that in terms of "time costs" the calculation exhibits decreasing returns to scale. This property is, of course, critical to the traditional economic issue of whether competitive markets can efficiently control activities such as collecting information. Furthermore, the formula exhibits tradeoffs between the size of the data n and the number of registers m, but there is a lower bound, $1 + \log_2 n$, on the delay involved in its calculation, whatever the number of computing registers.

6.4 Aggregating Preferences

Social choice rules are methods for aggregating individuals' preferences into collective action. Simplicity is particularly significant for a social choice rule because the rule has to be communicated to all members of the group. Social choice theory is not explicit about simplicity considerations, but such considerations underlie the theory. For example, one interpretation of Arrow's axiom of independence of irrelevant alternatives is that it expresses a simplicity requirement: The comparison between any two alternatives, a and b, must depend on agents' comparisons of only those two alternatives. The neutrality axiom is an even stronger condition of simplicity: It requires the existence of a unique principle on the basis of which comparisons between any two alternatives can be made.

The aim of the rest of this discussion is to clarify an intuition that the majority rule is a simple collective-decision rule. We will confine ourselves to the case of two social alternatives, 0 and 1. Preferences are assumed to be strict. A social choice rule is a function that attaches to each profile of 0's and 1's (where i's component is i's preferred outcome) a value, 0 or 1.

When considering the complexity of a social choice rule, imagine that the computation of the rule is carried out by a machine (finite automaton), $M = (Q, q^0, \mu, F)$, where Q is a set of states, q^0 is the initial state, $\mu(q, a)$ is the state that the machine moves to if it was in q and observes an input $a \in \{0, 1\}$, and F is a subset of states such that if the machine reaches any state in F, it stops with the answer 1. The information about the individuals' preferences is given as a sequence $x \in \{0, 1\}^{\{1,\ldots n\}}$. Starting with the state q^0, that machine moves to $q^{t+1} = \mu(q^t, x^t)$ and continues until it reaches either a state in F or the end of the input sequence. If the machine stops at F, the outcome is 1. In any other state, the outcome is 0. A machine M and a profile of votes x determine a unique outcome, $f_M(x)$.

Next we have to define what we mean by the complexity of a machine. In later chapters, we will focus on measuring complexity by the number of states in the machine. Here, we will take a different approach, similar to that discussed in Chapter 5, where we evaluated the complexity of perceptrons. The complexity of a machine is evaluated by the maximal complexity (order) of a state in the machine, independent of the number of states. The logic is similar to the one used to rank the complexity of perceptrons. Complexity here is linked to the ability to execute the basic operations of the machine and not to the number of times the operations are completed.

The states are ranked as follows: The simplest states, of order 0, are the absorbing states, those that do not even respond to the fact that an input has been read. A state of order 1 is one that triggers a transition to another state independently of the input content. A state of order 2 triggers the machine to move to another state only when it reads a specific input. A state of order 3 triggers a move to another state depending on the input it reads. An order 2 state is simpler than an order 3 state in the sense that an order 2 state searches for the one particular input that will trigger a transition, whereas an order 3 state responds differently to each of the two input bits it may receive.

q is of order	The condition
0	$\mu(q, a) \equiv q$ for any input a
1	$\mu(q, a) \equiv q'$ for all a $(q' \neq q)$
2	$\exists a^*$ so that $\mu(q, a^*) = q'$ $(q' \neq q)$ and $\mu(q, a) = q$ otherwise
3	$\exists q' \neq q''$ different from q, so that $\mu(q, 0) = q'$ and $\mu(q, 1) = q''$

For every social choice rule f, we can ask: What machine, M, is of the lowest complexity, so that $f_M = f$? We will now see that the machine that stops as soon as it identifies $[n/2]_+$ 1's is the simplest machine producing a social choice rule, f, that satisfies the consensus requirement that $f(1, 1, \ldots, 1) = 1$ and that is symmetric in the two alternatives, that is, $f(-x_1, \ldots, -x_n) = -f(x_1, \ldots, x_n)$ for any profile of opinions x, where the "−" stands for negation ($-1 = 0$ and $-0 = 1$).

Obviously any machine of complexity 1 produces constant social choice rules. For any complexity 2 machine, there must exist a sequence $(a_1, \ldots, a_K)$ with $0 \leq K \leq n$, so that the output of the machine with the input vector x is 1 if and only if x is of the form ([a block of $-a_1$], a_1, [a block of $-a_2$], a_2, \ldots, [a block of $-a_K$], a_K) (each block may be empty). For a complexity 2 machine M to satisfy the condition $f_M(1, \ldots, 1) = 1$, it must be that $(a_1, \ldots, a_K) = (1, \ldots, 1)$. That is, M's output is 1 if and only if there are at least K 1's in the vector x. Among these rules, the only one that treats the two alternatives symmetrically is the one with $K = [n/2]_+$, that is, majority rule.

6.5 Bibliographic Notes

Section 2 is based on Marschak and Radner (1972), with the exception of point (b), which is based on van Zandt (1996). Section 3 is a simplification of the model presented and analyzed in Radner (1993). Section 4 is inspired by Varian (1972).

For an overview of the subject, see Radner (1992).

6.6 Projects

1. *Innovative* Suggest an alternative definition of a team that will suit situations where more than one agent can activate an "output register" (like pulling a fire alarm).

2. *Innovative* In the model presented in Section 3, note an interesting difference between the operation $g_1(x, y) = \min\{x, y\}$ and the operation $g_2(x, y) = x + y$: Whereas $\min\{x, \min\{x, y\}\} = \min\{x, y\}$, it is not true that $x + (x + y) = x + y$. Explain why this difference does not influence the discussion in Section 3. Construct a model of organization in which such a difference will be significant (idea: consider the possibility of mistakes in the process).

3. *Reading* From the Gibbard-Satterthwaite theorem, we know that when the number of alternatives is larger than 2, nondictatorial social choice rules are exposed to the possibility of manipulation. Read Bartholdi, Tovey, and Trick (1989). Try to simplify their model in order to express the idea that complicated social choice rules are less easy to manipulate and thus may be desirable.

4. *Exercise* Study a variation of the model in Section 4 in which a machine is (Q, q_0, μ, λ), where λ is a function that assigns to each state an output, 0 or 1, with the interpretation that if the machine terminates reading the input vector when it is at the state q, the output of the machine is $\lambda(q)$. Characterize the set of machines of order 2 in this setup.

7   Modeling Bounded
Rationality in Games

7.1 Introduction

The discussion in previous chapters was confined to pure decision-theoretical situations. The second part of the book deals with the incorporation of procedural rationality considerations into models of interactive situations, mainly games. We focus on three bounded-rationality themes:

1. In standard game-theoretic analyses, each player behaves according to the rational man paradigm. In this chapter we study several models of interaction in which a player, when making a decision, follows a decision procedure that is not consistent with the rational man paradigm.

2. Even if the agents are rational, they may take into account procedural elements connected with their decision. For example, they may be concerned about the complexity of the strategy they employ. We show (Chapters 8 and 9) that the tradeoff between "optimality" and "complexity" can influence dramatically the outcome of the interaction in a class of repeated games.

3. The rational behavior of a player in a game requires his calculation of the other players' behavior. If the opponents are rational, the calculation of their actions requires working out the rational strategy of the first player. The self-referential nature of the concept of

"rationality" in interactive situations raises the question (discussed in Chapter 10) as to whether the limits on computability impose fundamental constraints on the existence of "rational strategies."

Many other issues of modeling bounded rationality in games will not be discussed in this book. Some of the omitted topics have counterparts in decision theory (such as the limits on information processing and imperfect recall), and some are unique to game theory (for instance, the ability of a player to analyze his opponents' behavior).

In the course of the discussion, I will refer to two different interpretations of game theoretical solutions. Under one interpretation, a player is an agent who operates in an environment determined by the other agents' behavior and who takes the behavior of the other agents as an input to his decision problem. Under this interpretation, a solution describes a player's behavior when he takes the other agents' behavior as "known." Under the other interpretation, a solution strategy entails the behavior of a player who does not know the other players' strategies but reasons about them from the model's primitives (i.e., the preferences and the informational structures). These two different interpretations of equilibrium produces tension into any game theoretical discussion, and is unavoidable once bounded rationality elements have been introduced into the model.

7.2 Interactions Between Luce Players

The model introduced in this section is based on Luce's model of choice. The model describes behavior that is stochastic in a systematic way. Let $\mathbf{A}$ be a space of alternatives. The decision maker attaches to each alternative $a \in \mathbf{A}$ a non-negative number $v(a)$ so that given a set of alternatives $A \subseteq \mathbf{A}$, he selects each action a^* from A with probability $v(a^*)/\Sigma_{a \in A} v(a)$. For the case where the set $\mathbf{A}$ is the set of lotteries over a set of consequences C, the function v has a more detailed structure. There are value numbers, $(u(c))_{c \in C}$, attached to each of the possible consequences so that $v(L)$ is the expected u-value of the lottery L. When the decision maker chooses from the set of lotteries A, he chooses the lottery $L^* \in A$ with probability $v(L^*)/\Sigma_{L \in A} v(L)$. Note that "Luce numbers" are interpreted differently from von Neumann-Morgenstern (vNM) utilities.

Our interest in Luce's model is not due to its attractiveness. Although Luce provided an axiomatization for this theory, its appeal from a procedural point of view remains to be substantiated. Luce's theory is used here only as a tool for demonstrating how the Nash equilibrium type of analysis can be applied to decision theories other than vNM expected utility maximization.

Consider a situation where each player $i \in N$ has to choose an action from a finite set of actions A_i and where his choice adheres to Luce's theory. Player i bases his decision on a function, u_i, which assigns a non-negative number, $u_i(a)$, to every possible outcome $a \in \times_{i \in N} A_i$. For any vector σ_{-i} of mixed strategies for all players except i, any action $a_i \in A_i$ induces a lottery; the expected value of this lottery is $u_i(a_i, \sigma_{-i}) = \Sigma_{a_{-i}} u_i(a_i, a_{-i}) \Pi_{j \neq i} \sigma_j(a_j)$. Player i's choice is a mixed strategy, σ_i, in which the ratio between the probabilities of any two possible actions, a_i and a_i', is equal to the ratio between $u_i(a_i, \sigma_{-i})$ and $u_i(a_i', \sigma_{-i})$. An *equilibrium* is a profile of mixed strategies, $(\sigma_i^*)_{i \in N}$, such that for all i and for all $a_i \in A_i$, $\sigma_i^*(a_i) = u_i(a_i, \sigma_{-i}^*)/\Sigma_{\alpha \in A_i} u_i(a, \sigma_{-i}^*)$; that is, given the other players' strategies, σ_{-i}^*, player i's choice is σ_{-i}^*. A straightforward application of Brouer's fixed point theorem guarantees the existence of an equilibrium.

Note that in this model, the only way that an action gets a zero weight in equilibrium is if it yields a zero payoff. Thus, the game

	C	D
C	2, 2	0, 3
D	3, 0	1, 1

which looks like the Prisoner's Dilemma, has two equilibria. One is the regular Nash equilibrium, and the other (more interesting one) is the mixed strategy equilibrium in which each player takes action C with probability $1/4$. Adding a constant $\varepsilon > 0$ to all payoffs will change the set of equilibria: the pure equilibrium disappears and the unique equilibrium, when ε goes to infinity, converges to $\sigma_i^* = (1/2, 1/2)$ for both i.

7.3   A Game with Procedurally Rational Players

In this section, we analyze the interaction between players who use a decision procedure whose primitives include the players' preferences on the set of outcomes, but differs from that of the rational man. Here, a decision maker, when having to choose from a set of actions A with uncertain consequences in a set C, constructs a deterministic action–consequence relationship and takes the action with the best attached consequence. The chance that a certain consequence $c \in C$ will be attached to $a \in A$ is taken to be the frequency with which c is observed with a. Thus, the action–consequence relationship, being random, yields random behavior.

To demonstrate, assume that action a leads, with equal probabilities, to the monetary consequences \$0 or \$2, whereas action b leads, with equal probabilities, to the consequences \$1 or \$3. Assume that the payoffs from the two actions are independent. Then, with probability $1/4$, the decision maker attaches to action a the consequence \$2 and to action b the consequence \$1, and thus chooses a; any of the other three possible action–consequence relationships leads to the choice of b. Thus, the behavior induced from this procedure will be the choice of a with probability $1/4$ and b with probability $3/4$.

The simplest version of this game model applies to a symmetric two-player game, (A, u), where each player has to choose an action from a set A; his payoff, if he chooses the action $x \in A$ and his opponent chooses the action $y \in A$, is $u(x, y)$. A candidate for the solution is a mixed strategy α^* (a lottery on A). Given α^*, for each $x \in A$, let $L(x, \alpha^*)$ be the lottery that induces the consequence $u(x, y)$ with the probability $\alpha^*(y)$. Our equilibrium requirement is that for all $a \in A$, the number $\alpha^*(a)$ is the probability that the action a gets the highest value from among all independent realizations of $\{L(x, \alpha^*)\}_{x \in A}$, breaking ties evenly among all actions that yield the maximal payoff.

Unlike the rational player in game theory, in this model, a player does not start by constructing a conjecture about his opponent's action. Instead, he links each of his possible actions to a consequence. When doing so, he does not take into account any strategic considerations of the other players.

Example 1 To illustrate the solution concept, let us calculate the equilibria of the symmetric game with $A = \{a, b\}$ and the utility function given in the table:

	a	b
a	2	4
b	3	1

Denote $p = \alpha^*(a)$. The probability that $L(a, \alpha^*)$ will be higher than $L(b, \alpha^*)$ is $p(1 - p) + (1 - p)$. Thus, in equilibrium, $p = p(1 - p) + (1 - p)$; that is, $\alpha^*(a) = (\sqrt{5} - 1)/2 \approx 0.62$.

This equilibrium concept has two interpretations. For the "real experimentation interpretation," imagine the existence of a large population of individuals, pairs of which are occasionally matched and interact. Upon joining the population, a new arrival does the following: he samples every action once and attaches to each action the consequence he obtained. Then, he chooses forever the action that yields the best consequence. Under this interpretation, an equilibrium corresponds to a steady state in which the probability that a new player chooses a certain action is equal to the fraction of the population associated with that action.

An alternative interpretation, preferable to my mind, takes the experimentation idea less concretely. A player forms an action-consequence linkage in a mental process. The probability that he attaches consequence c to action a is not arbitrary; it is assumed that the attachment reflects the true (probably stochastic) pattern according to which his opponent plays the game. It is assumed that he attaches consequence (a, b) to action a with the probability by which action b is taken.

Note that the equilibrium notion we are talking about requires the full specification of each player's ranking of *all* the outcomes, whereas the standard notion of a pure Nash equilibrium requires that each player rank the outcomes exclusively for a fixed opponent's action.

It is easy to see (using Brouer's fixed point theorem) that for finite games, the existence of an equilibrium is guaranteed.

Example 2 Assume that $A = \{a, b\}$ and that the action a weakly dominates the action b, with $u(a, a) > u(b, a)$ and $u(a, b) = u(b, b)$, so that the game can be written as

	a	b
a	1	x
b	0	x

Note that we have here five different games (according to whether $x > 1$, $x = 1$, $0 < x < 1$, $x = 0$ and $x < 0$). Let α^* be an equilibrium and $p = \alpha^*(a)$. The conclusion that $p = 1$ follows from the fact that for all values of x, $1 - p \le (1 - p)^2/2 + p(1 - p)$. To see this inequality, note that the action b can be selected only if:

- b ties with a, because the consequence x is attached to both actions,
- $x \geq 1$ and the consequence 1 is attached to the action a and the consequence x to b, or
- $x \leq 0$ and x is attached to action a and 0 to action b.

Example 3 Consider the case where a weakly dominates b and $u(a, a) = u(b, a)$, that is, the game is one of the five games having the structure:

	a	b
a	x	1
b	x	0

Then, the unique Nash equilibrium outcome, $\alpha^*(a) = 1$, is never an equilibrium.

Example 4 For two-action games, if a strictly dominates b, the only equilibrium is $\alpha^*(a) = 1$ (confirm!). However, for symmetric games with more than two actions, the dominated action can appear in equilibrium with positive probability. Consider the game:

	a	b	c
a	2	5	8
b	1	4	7
c	0	3	6

This game carries the interpretation of a voluntary exchange game between two traders, each holding two units of a good worth 1 to the initial holder and 3 to the other. The game has two equilibria: one is the pure strategy equilibrium, $\alpha^*(a) = 1$ (with no trade); the second is approximately (0.52, 0.28, 0.20), in which both dominated actions occur with positive probability.

The extension of the solution concept to asymmetric situations is straightforward. It allows the application of the concept to an extensive game through its normal form.

Example 5 Consider the single-round version of the centipede game (fig. 7.1) which has the reduced normal form:

	S	C
S	1 0	1 0
C	0 3	2 2

Denote by p and q the probabilities that players 1 and 2, respectively, stop the game. For (p, q) to be an equilibrium, it has to be that $p = q$ (player 1's action S wins only if player 1 attaches the consequence 0 to the action C) and $q = (1 - p) + p^2/2$. Thus in equilibrium $p = q = 2 - \sqrt{2}$.

In the T-round centipede game, there are two players, alternating in order, each of whom has an opportunity to stop the game. Available to each player are $T + 1$ plans ("always continue" and "stop at the tth opportunity" for $t = 1, 2, \ldots , T$). The preferences have the property that at each history it is best for the player who has to move to stop the game if and only if he expects that in the event he continues the game will end at the next stage (by the other player stopping the game or by the termination of the game).

An interesting fact about the T-round centipede game is that when the number of periods goes to infinity, the equilibrium (as

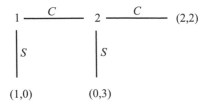

Figure 7.1

defined in this section) probability that player 1 stops the game immediately goes to 0! To see this, denote by p the probability that player 1 stops the game at the first period and by q the probability that player 2 chooses to stop the game at his first opportunity. Player 1's strategy of stopping at the first period is the winner only if he attaches to his other T strategies the consequence associated with player 2 stopping the game immediately. Thus $p = q^T$. Player 2's strategy of stopping at the first node (if reached) is the winner with a probability that does not exceed $(1 - p) + p^{T+1}/(T + 1)$ because for this strategy to win it is necessary that player 2 attaches to stopping a scenario that involves player 1's not stopping the game earlier (probability $1 - p$) or that he attaches to the consequence that player 1 stops the game at the first period to all his $T + 1$ strategies (a case where all his $T + 1$ strategies tie). It is simple to verify that for every $\varepsilon > 0$, there is a T^* large enough so that if (p, q) is a solution of $p = q^T$ and $q \le (1 - p) + p^{T+1}/(T + 1)$ and if $T \ge T^*$ then $p \le \varepsilon$.

This result is appealing as a potential resolution of the paradoxical aspects of the centipede game. But notice that this argument follows from treating the game as a strategic game, losing information included in the extensive game. Going back to the single-round version of the game (Example 5), player 2 finds the strategy "continue" to be better than the strategy "stop" only when he attaches the scenario that player 1 has already stopped the game to "stop" and he attaches the scenario that player 1 did not stop the game to "continue." A more natural mode of reasoning for player 2 in Example 5 would involve his taking into account the facts which forced him to move; that is, that player 1 has not stopped the game. The solution concept described in this section, because it applies only to the strategic game, misses this point.

7.4 Limited Foresight in Extensive Games

One of the most interesting modeling issues in the study of games with boundedly rational players is that of modeling players who have limited ability to understand the extensive game they face. The game of chess is a good example for illustrating some of our concerns. In game theoretical terms, chess is a finite, zero-sum, two-player game with perfect information. At the outset of the game, one of the players ("white") has to make a move, and at each of the subsequent histories, the other player ("black") has to move, and so on, in alternating order. Attached to each of the terminal histories is one of three consequences: "white wins," "black wins," and "draw." The preferences of the players are naturally defined. Chess has a finite number of histories because of the rule stating that if the same position is repeated three times in the course of a play, then the outcome of that play is a draw.

At the beginning of the twentieth century, Zermelo proved a proposition which can be interpreted, "chess is a trivial game." To see this we can use the *backward induction technique:* Assign to each history h a number, $d(h)$, which is the length of the longest path from h to one of the terminal histories. A history h with $d(h) = 0$ is a terminal history. Assign a "value," $v(h)$, to each terminal history h, equal to the consequence attached to that history. Continue inductively. At each history h, with $d(h) = d$, one player, i, has to choose from a finite number of actions. Each action a_i leads to the history (h, a_i) with $d(h, a_i) \leq d - 1$, for which we have already assigned a value. Define player i's strategy at h to be an action, a_i^*, so that $v(h, a_i^*)$ is at least as good for player i as any other $v(h, a_i)$. Set $v(h) = v(h, a_i^*)$. This procedure ends after a finite number of steps. The value of the game is the value assigned to the initial history. The procedure also constructs a pair of strategies that can easily be shown to form a (subgame perfect) equilibrium. Furthermore, because the game is a zero-sum game, each of these strategies has the property that its holder can make sure that *whatever* his opponent does, the outcome of the game will be at least as good for him as the game's value. That is, if the value of the game is "white wins," then the strategy that we have just defined ensures white's victory.

If the value of the game is "black wins," then black can assure himself to win. If the value is a draw, each player can employ a strategy that would secure him at least a draw.

The striking fact about chess is that although we can easily *prove* that the game has a value, we can calculate neither that value nor the maxmin strategies. In the preceding proof we assumed that each player, when making a choice at a particular history of the game, is able to calculate correctly the consequences following each of his possible actions. But this calculation requires going through a huge number of steps, something no human being can accomplish. By the way, it might still be the case that chess will one day be "solved" without applying the backward induction technique, but by some bright idea based on a thorough understanding of the game.

A maxmin strategy is not necessarily the rational strategy to follow. If the value of chess is a draw, the case may be that when playing against a weak player, a player will do better by using another strategy, one allowing him to win. Note that even if the value of chess were known, people would not necessarily stop playing the game, just as they continue to play a simple game like tic-tac-toe despite its value being a draw. The fact that the maxmin strategies are known does not mean that everyone is familiar with a specific maxmin strategy or able to execute it.

Much has been said about the way people and computer programs play chess (or similar board games). It seems that people typically "check out" several likely scenarios and that they entertain some method to evaluate the endpoint of each scenario (like counting the pieces in chess). People differ in the depth of their inquiry, the quality of the "typical scenarios" selected, and the way they evaluate their endpoint positions. They also exhibit differences in the ways in which they make mistakes. (Actually, it is not at all clear that mistakes are necessarily bad; for example, sometimes a less conventional move can throw an opponent off balance.)

Modeling "chesslike" behavior in games is still a puzzle. I am not aware of any analytical model that deals satisfactorily with this issue. I will make do with demonstrating some of the modeling difficulties by using a very special case of an extensive game with perfect information (and a chance player) having the following payoff structure: A profile of payoffs is attached to each action and each player's payoff at a terminal history is the sum of the payoffs he collected along the history.

Assume that each player's foresight horizon is K. This means that he decides what his behavior will be at each history solely on the basis of considerations regarding the next K periods. How does he go about it? Here are two possible approaches. Common to both approaches is the assumption that at each history a player compares scenarios within the foreseen horizon by weighting the sums of payoffs he expects to collect in the next K moves of the game.

Under one approach, an equilibrium is a profile of strategies, $(f_i^*)_{i \in N}$, such that for all i and for any history h in which player i has to move, $f_i^*(h)$ is the *action* that leads to the maximization of the sum of payoffs at the foreseen horizon, given the equilibrium actions taken *both* by the player and his opponent, in the histories found within distance K from the history h. Thus, under this approach, each player at every history in which he has to move is analyzed as if he were an autonomous player who moves only once and has preferences represented by the sum of his payoffs in the foreseen K stages of the game. This analysis is in the spirit of Strotz's treatment of decision problems with changing tastes, discussed earlier in the context of imperfect recall.

To demonstrate this approach, consider the following one-player extensive game:

Example 1 A decision maker has at each period the option of taking one of two possible actions, 0 or 1. At period t, the action 0 yields the stage payoff 0, whereas the action 1 yields the stage payoff δ^t, where $\delta > 1$ (!). To make the game stop in finite time, assume that at each period the "game" may cease with probability $\varepsilon > 0$ (where ε is "small"). Assume that the decision maker's horizon is $K = 2$. The following strategy is an equilibrium: The decision maker chooses 1 if and only if the length of the consecutive string of previous 0's is odd. This strategy produces the path $(0, 1, 0, 1, \ldots)$. After a history in which this strategy calls for him to take the action 0, the decision maker does not do better by taking the action 1, since if he takes the action 1 he expects to take the action 0 one period later, and the string of payoffs $(0, \delta^{t+1})$ is better for him than the string of payoffs $(\delta^t, 0)$. When he has to take the action 1, he expects the string $(1, 0)$, which is better for him than the path $(0, 0)$, which is the path expected if the action 0 is taken.

Under a second approach, player i, at the history h in which he has to move, takes an action that constitutes the first step of a strategy that maximizes player i's sum of payoffs in the next K stages, taking as given the *other* players' behaviors in his foreseen horizon and absent any restrictions on his own planned actions. The equilibrium concept that fits the second approach is a profile of strategies, $(f_i^*)_{i \in N}$, such that for every history h, after which player i has to move, we have $f_i^*(h) = f_i(h)$, where f_i is some strategy that maximizes the sum of the payoffs in the K horizon given the other players' strategies.

There is no reason to expect that this type of equilibrium will yield an optimal strategy. Even for a single-agent decision problem, this approach does not necessarily lead to a "good path" as the player might enter a "trap" he has not perceived.

Going back to Example 1, according to the second approach, the only equilibrium is for the decision maker always to choose the action 1. To appreciate the differences between the two equilibrium concepts, let us review one more example.

Example 2   Consider a two-player situation where the players alternately choose one of two actions, G (for "giving") or NG (for "not giving"). Assume that the "stage" payoffs are such that if the player who has to move chooses G, he loses 2 units of payoff and the other player gets 3; if he chooses NG, both get a payoff of 0. Assume that at each stage, there is probability ε that the game ends (where ε is positive and "small").

Consider the model with $K = 3$. Let (f_1^*, f_2^*) be the pair of strategies defined by $f_i^*(h) = NG$ if the history h contains at least one play of NG, and $f_i^*(h) = G$ otherwise. To see that (f_1^*, f_2^*) is an equilibrium according to the second approach, consider a history after which player i has to move. First, assume that in h, the action NG was chosen at least once. Player i then anticipates that irrespective of what he does, player j will play NG at the next period; thus, his best plan for the forthcoming three periods is to play NG in the first and the third periods. Next, assume that the history h is a constant play of G. Player i anticipates that if he chooses G in the first period within his horizon, player j will play G as well, and thus he can achieve the stream $(-2, 3, 0)$. If he plays NG at the first period, player j will play NG as well, and he will be able to obtain only the inferior stream of payoffs $(0, 0, 0)$.

This pair of strategies, (f_1^*, f_2^*), is not an equilibrium according to the first approach. The optimality of playing G was based on player i's plan to choose NG at the third period, though he will actually choose G. By the first approach, player i has the "correct expectations" about himself if he plays G, which leads to the stream $(-2, +3, -2)$, which is inferior to the stream $(0, 0, 0)$ that follows if he chooses NG.

To conclude, I believe that the two approaches fall short of capturing the spirit of limited-foresight reasoning. By the first approach, a player treats his future behavior as given, though he can influence it. By the second approach, he treats the other players' plans as known, though he does not know his own moves. Modeling games with limited foresight remains a great challenge.

7.5 Bibliographic Notes

Section 2 is based on Chen, Friedman, and Thisse (1997); see also related earlier work by Rosenthal (1989) and McKelvey and Palfrey (1995). Section 3 is based on Osborne and Rubinstein (1997). The last part of Section 4 is based on ideas that emerged from a research project jointly conducted with Asher Wolinsky. Jehiel (1995) analyzes the multiselves approach with respect to a family of alternating-moves games with "limited foresight." For Luce's choice model, see Luce (1959).

7.6 Projects

1. *Innovative* Consider a scenario where two prisoners who were arrested on January 1 decide to coordinate an escape on the morning of April 13. They have been placed in two separate cells. They do not have a calendar or any writing device, but they can observe every sunrise. During the first few days, they keep track of the exact date and are certain that their calculations are correct. But as time passes, their degree of confidence diminishes. Try to model this situation in game theoretic terms. Compare it with the situation where a single prisoner has to escape by himself on April 13.

2. *Innovative* Read the axiomatization of Luce's decision theory (see Luce (1959)) and try to give the axioms procedural interpretations.

3. *Reading* Read Rosenthal (1989) and McKelvey and Palfrey (1995), and compare the decision procedure there with that of Chen, Friedman, and Thisse (1997).

4. *Exercise* Consider the effect of duplicating an action in the two game theoretic models discussed in Sections 2 and 3. Provide an interpretation for your findings.

5. *Exercise* (Based on Chen, Friedman, and Thisse [1997].) Consider a modification of the Luce model: Player i's behavior is a mixed strategy, σ_i, in which the ratio between the probabilities of any two possible actions, a_i and a_i', is equal to the ratio between $u_i(a_i, \sigma_{-i})^\mu$ and $u_i(a_i', \sigma_{-i})^\mu$. Provide an interpretation for the μ coefficient and, in particular, for $\mu = 0$ and a "very high" μ.

6. *Exercise* (Based on Osborne and Rubinstein (1997).) Consider the model of a game with procedurally rational players, as described in Section 3, in regard to a situation where two sellers of a commodity "Bertrand compete" in the market. Denote by $0 < p_1 < p_2 \ldots < p_K < 1$ the K possible prices. Denote by $u(p, p')$ the profit

of a seller who charges the price p when his opponent charges the price p'. Assume that the set of prices is dense enough that $u(p_k, p_k) < u(p_{k-1}, p_k)$ for each $k \geq 2$. Show that the only equilibrium in this model is for the two sellers to charge p_1.

7. *Exercise* For the class of symmetric games, analyze the procedure in which each player "samples once" his opponent's action and takes a best response to this action. Define an equilibrium concept and examine some examples.

8 Complexity Considerations in Repeated Games

8.1 Introduction

In this chapter, we will incorporate a special type of procedural consideration into the model of repeated games. We will see that when players take this procedural consideration into account, the analysis is changed dramatically.

At the heart of our discussion in this chapter is the tradeoff often facing a decision maker when choosing a strategy. On one hand, he hopes his strategy will serve his goals; on the other hand, he would like it to be as simple as possible. There are many reasons why a player may value simplicity: a more complex plan of action is more likely to break down, is more difficult to learn, and may require more time to be implemented. We will not examine these reasons here but simply assume that complexity is costly and under the control of the player.

One may study the interaction of agents who account for the complexity of their rule of behavior in the context of any model. It is particularly appropriate in the context of an extensive game, where a strategy determines a player's actions in various circumstances and thus can be viewed as a rule of behavior. Within the set of extensive games, we will study the model of infinitely repeated games. There are several reasons for this choice. First, the model allows the use of strategies that are intuitively very simple, as well as those that are intuitively very complicated. Thus, the tradeoff between the optimality and the simplicity of the strategies would seem to be significant. The second is the popularity of this model in economics and other social sciences. But, most important, it works—that is to say, the analysis does yield rich results.

8.2 The Model of the Repeated Game: A Brief Review

The model of repeated games relates to situations in which each player takes into account the effect of *his* "current" behavior on the *other* players' "future" behavior. The model allows us to examine the logic of long-term interactions. Its aim is to explain phenomena such as cooperation, revenge, and threats.

The basic point of the analysis of the repeated game model is illustrated by the scenario in which two individuals repeatedly play the Prisoner's Dilemma.

	C	D
C	3, 3	0, 4
D	4, 0	1, 1

Action D strictly dominates action C for each player, thus the stage game has a unique Nash equilibrium in which each player chooses D. If the game is played repeatedly, then the mutually desirable outcome (C, C) can be sustained under the condition that each player believes that a defection will result in an eventual loss that outweighs the immediate gain.

When studying a repeated game (with perfect information), we have in mind a scenario in which the players play a basic strategic game at each period (which we will refer to as the one-shot game). In each period all the players simultaneously choose an action available in the one-shot game. At the end of each period, the actions taken by the players are revealed.

We distinguish between *infinitely* and *finitely* repeated games. The difference lies in whether the players are aware of the existence of a final period of interaction. The naive interpretation of the infinitely repeated game is that of a one-shot game played indefinitely. However, a preferable interpretation is that of a game in which after each period the players believe that the interaction will continue for an additional period. Even if a game really does have a terminal period, the model of an infinitely repeated game is appropriate, in my opinion, when the players do not incorporate the existence of that endpoint into their strategic reasoning. In contrast, a finitely repeated game is an appropriate model when the players assign a special status to the endpoint in their strategic considerations.

The two models are very different. The existence of an endpoint is a crucial factor in the analysis of the finitely repeated game. For example, it is easy to see that the *finitely* repeated Prisoner's Dilemma, in which a player's payoff is the accumulated sum of the G-payoffs in the T periods, has a unique Nash equilibrium outcome (as well as a unique subgame perfect equilibrium) that constitutes the constant repetition of (D, D), independently of T. In contrast, the infinitely repeated game may exhibit equilibria of a very different nature, including a constant play of the (C, C) outcome.

In this chapter we deal mainly with the infinitely repeated model. The cornerstone of this model is a one-shot strategic game, $G = (N, \{A_i\}_{i \in N}, \{u_i\}_{i \in N})$. For the sake of simplicity, we confine ourselves to the case of two-player games so that the set of players is taken to be $N = \{1, 2\}$. A_i is the set of i's actions. Player i's payoff is represented by a utility function, $u_i: A_1 \times A_2 \to \mathbf{R}$. The utility numbers will soon become the basis for the construction of time preferences. A G-outcome is a member of $A = A_1 \times A_2$.

A *strategy of player i* in the repeated game is a function that assigns an action in A_i to every finite sequence $(a^1, \ldots, a^t)$ of G-outcomes.

In order to complete the description of the infinitely repeated game model, we must specify the players' preferences on infinite sequences of G-outcomes. It is assumed that each player i evaluates a sequence of G-outcomes (a^t) by applying an evaluation criterion to the induced sequence of utility numbers $(u_i(a^t))$. We will discuss two types of evaluation criteria:

Discounting There is some number $\delta \in (0, 1)$ (the *discount factor*) such that the sequence (v_i^t) is evaluated by $\Sigma_t \delta^t v_i^t$. We refer to $(1 - \delta)(\Sigma_t \delta^{t-1} v_i^t)$ as player i's repeated game payoff in the repeated game with discounting.

Limit of means A sequence (v_i^t) is evaluated by its limiting average, $\lim_{T \to \infty} \Sigma_{t=1,...,T} v_i^t / T$. (In the following analysis we will not have to be concerned with the possibility that this limit may not be well defined.) We refer to this limit as player i's repeated game payoff in the repeated game with limit of means.

Notice that the discounting criterion assigns diminishing importance to payoffs the later they are realized, whereas the criterion of the limit of means treats all periods symmetrically. Any change in the payoff in any single period affects the discounted sum. In contrast, the limit of means criterion ignores payoff differences in any finite number of periods.

Within the theory of repeated games, the fundamental results are the *Folk Theorems*. These are characterizations of the payoff vectors that can be sustained as an outcome of a Nash equilibrium. The Folk Theorems show that a huge set of outcomes (including, for example, the repeated play of the cooperative outcome in the Prisoner's Dilemma) can be sustained in equilibrium.

For a description of the basic Folk Theorem we require some notation. Denote by $u(a)$ the pair $(u_i(a))_{i \in N}$. We call a vector $v \in \mathbf{R}^N$ a *payoff profile* of G if there is an $a \in A$ so that $v_i = u_i(a)$ for both i. A vector $v \in \mathbf{R}^2$ is a *feasible payoff profile* of G if it is a convex combination of payoff profiles of outcomes in G, that is, if $v = \Sigma_{a \in A} \alpha_a u(a)$ for some collection $\{\alpha_a\}_{a \in A}$ of non-negative rational numbers α_a with $\Sigma_{a \in A} \alpha_a = 1$. (In the literature, the coefficients α_a are allowed to be any real, not necessarily rational numbers. This generalization slightly complicates the argument without adding any substance.)

Player i's *minmax payoff* in G, henceforth denoted by v_i, is the lowest payoff that the other player, j, can force upon player i:

$$v_i = \min_{a_j \in A_j} \max_{a_i \in A_i} u_i(a_j, a_i).$$

A payoff profile w in G for which $w_i \geq v_i$ for both $i \in N$ is called *enforceable*; if $w_i > v_i$ for both $i \in N$, then w is *strictly enforceable*. Denote by $\sigma_{-i} \in A_j$ a solution for the minmaximization problem, that is, σ_{-i} is a most severe punishment strategy of j against i.

It is easy to see that if v is a payoff vector of some Nash equilibrium (for the repeated game with either evaluation criterion), v must be feasible and enforceable. This fact, together with the following, more interesting result, comprises the essence of the Folk Theorem.

Proposition 8.1 Let w be an enforceable feasible payoff profile of G. There is a Nash equilibrium of the repeated game with a limit of the means which induces w as a payoff vector.

A proof of this proposition is very simple. It reduces to the construction of a pair of strategies which can be shown to be a Nash equilibrium of the repeated game. In such a pair of strategies, the players cyclically play a sequence of outcomes that, on average, yield the vector w. As soon as a deviation is made by any of the players, the other will forever "minmax" the deviator.

In the case of discounting, we have to be a little more careful with the details but the same proposition essentially holds for a "large enough" discount factor (its proof is left as an exercise).

Proposition 8.2 Let w be a strictly enforceable feasible payoff profile of G. For all $\varepsilon > 0$, there is some δ' such that for any $\delta > \delta'$, there exists a payoff profile w' of G for which $|w'_i - w_i| < \varepsilon$ for both i and w' is a payoff profile of a Nash equilibrium of the discounted infinitely repeated game of G.

Thus, the Folk Theorems confirm that socially desirable outcomes that cannot be sustained if players are short-sighted, can be sustained in equilibrium if the players have long-term objectives.

One of the difficulties with the proof of the Folk Theorem is that the profile of strategies used may involve threats that are not credible. Although this does not occur in the Prisoner's Dilemma, a situation may occur in Nash equilibrium where one player is supposed to respond to another player's deviation by means of a noncredible punishment plan. The requirement that punishment threats be credible is expressed by the notion of subgame perfect equilibrium. Apparently, the Folk Theorems continue to hold even when the term "Nash equilibrium" is replaced by the term "subgame perfect equilibrium" (for the discounting case, it requires a weak constraint on the set of games). We will not expand on this point; the reader can find an extensive discussion of the issue in any modern book on game theory.

Note that Folk Theorems are statements about the payoff vectors that can be sustained in equilibrium. However, the institutions that sustain equilibria are not exhibited by the equilibrium payoff vectors themselves but by the equilibrium *strategies*. Understanding the logic of long-term interactions requires, in my opinion, the characterization of the equilibrium *strategy scheme*. In referring to a strategy scheme, I am alluding to its structure, stripped of the details arising from the particular payoff to be supported. The repeated-games literature has made little progress toward this target.

In the rest of this chapter, we will seek ways to refine the huge set of Nash equilibria and to derive necessary conditions on the equilibrium strategies by appending to the players the desire to reduce the complexity of their strategy. In order to reach these targets, we will first replace the notion of a "strategy" with the notion of a "machine."

8.3 Strategies as Machines in Infinitely Repeated Games

At this point, we depart from the conventional literature on repeated games and replace the notion of a strategy with that of a *machine*. A machine is meant to be an abstraction of the process by which a player *implements* a rule of behavior in a repeated game.

A *machine (finite automaton)* for player i in an infinitely repeated game of G is a four-tuple $(Q_i, q_i^0, f_i, \tau_i)$ where

Q_i is a *finite* set of *states,*

$q_i^0 \in Q_i$ is the *initial state,*

$f_i: Q_i \to A_i$ is an *output function* that assigns an action to every state, and

$\tau_i: Q_i \times A_j \to Q_i$ is the *transition function* that assigns a state to every pair of a state and an action of the other player.

The set Q_i is unrestricted. From the point of view of the definition of a machine, the names of the states have no significance. The fact that we call a state "cooperative," for example, does not mean that the behavior associated with it is in fact cooperative; however, we will attempt to attach names to states that correspond to their intuitive meaning.

A machine operates as follows: In the first period, the state is q_i^0 and the machine chooses the action $f_i(q_i^0)$. If a_j is the action chosen by the other player in the first period, then the state of player i's machine changes to $\tau_i(q_i^0, a_j)$ and, in the second period, player i chooses the action dictated by f_i in this state. The state again changes according to the transition function, given the other player's action, and the process continues. Thus, whenever the machine is in some state q, it chooses the action $f_i(q)$ while the transition function, τ_i, specifies the machine's move from q (to a state) in response to the action taken by the other player.

Note that the transition function depends only on the present state and the other player's action. This formalization fits the natural description of a strategy as player i's plan of action, in all possible circumstances, that are consistent with player i's plans. This interpretation of a strategy well suits our purposes in this chapter. In contrast, the notion of a game theoretic strategy for player i requires the specification of an action for any possible history, including those that are inconsistent with player i's plan of action. The game theoretic notion of a strategy is required in order to allow the application of the notion of subgame perfect equilibrium. The definition of Nash equilibrium, however, requires only the specification of behavior following histories that are *consistent* with a player's rule of behavior. (As an aside, in order to formulate a "game theoretic strategy" as an automaton, the only change required is to construct the transition function such that $\tau_i: Q_i \times A \rightarrow Q_i$ rather than $\tau_i: Q_i \times A_j \rightarrow Q_i$.)

The following are several machines available to a player in the repeated Prisoner's Dilemma game.

Example 1 The following machine $(Q_i, q_i^0, f_i, \tau_i)$ carries out the ("grim") strategy that chooses C so long as both players have chosen C in every period in the past, and chooses D otherwise.

$Q_i = \{q_C, q_D\}$.

$q_i^0 = q_C$.

$f_i(q_C) = C$ and $f_i(q_D) = D$.

$$\tau_i(q, a_j) = \begin{cases} q_C & (q, a_j) = (q_C, C) \\ q_D & \text{otherwise.} \end{cases}$$

This machine is illustrated in the figure 8.1. Each circle corresponds to a state; the name of the action taken at that state appears below

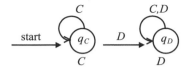

Figure 8.1

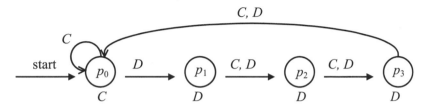

Figure 8.2

each circle. The initial state is indicated by an arrow. The arrows correspond to the transitions.

This machine is, of course, not the only one which implements the "grim" strategy, but it is certainly the most natural and, in some sense, the simplest.

Example 2 Player 1's machine M_1, shown in figure 8.2, plays C as long as player 2 plays C and plays D for three periods if player 2 plays D when the machine is in state q_C. After three periods, the machine reverts to state p_0, whatever actions the other player takes. (We can think of the other player as being "punished" for playing D for three periods and then "forgiven.") Notice that a machine must have at least four states in order to carry out this strategy.

Example 3 The machine M_2, shown in figure 8.3, starts by playing C. The machine continues to play C if the other player chooses D. If the other player chooses C, then M_2 switches to q_1 and plays D until the other player chooses D, at which time M_2 reverts to q_0.

In order to illustrate the evolution of play in a repeated game in which each player's strategy is carried out by a machine, suppose

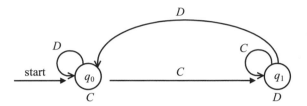

Figure 8.3

that player 1 uses the machine M_1 and player 2 uses the machine M_2. The machines start in the states p_0 and q_0, respectively. The outcome in the first period is (C, C) because the output function of M_1 assigns the action C to state p_0 and the output function of M_2 assigns the action C to state q_0. The states in the following period are determined by the transition functions. The transition function of M_1 leaves the machine in state p_0 because the outcome in the first period was (C, C), whereas the transition function of M_2 moves the machine from q_0 to q_1 in response to this input. Thus, the pair of states in period 2 is (p_0, q_1). The output functions determine the outcome in period 2 to be (C, D), so that M_1 moves from p_0 to p_1 and M_2 remains in q_1. The play continues through period 6 according to the following table:

Period	State of M_1	State of M_2	Outcome	Payoff vector
1	p_0	q_0	(C, C)	3, 3
2	p_0	q_1	(C, D)	0, 4
3	p_1	q_1	(D, D)	1, 1
4	p_2	q_0	(D, C)	4, 0
5	p_3	q_0	(D, C)	4, 0
6	p_0	q_0	(C, C)	3, 3

In period 6, the pair of states is the same as it was in period 1; the states and outcomes then continue to cycle in this manner. The fact that cycles are generated is obviously not peculiar to this example—

whenever each player uses a finite state machine, a cycle is eventually attained, though it may not necessarily start at period 1.

Generally, every pair (M_1, M_2) of machines induces a sequence $(a^t(M_1, M_2))_{t=1,2,...}$ of outcomes of G and a sequence $(q^t(M_1, M_2))_{t=1,2,...}$ of pairs of states defined as follows:

$$q_i^1(M_1, M_2) = q_i^0$$

$$a_i^t(M_1, M_2) = f_i(q_i^t(M_1, M_2))$$

$$q_i^{t+1}(M_1, M_2) = \tau_i(q_i^t(M_1, M_2), a_j^t(M_1, M_2)) \text{ (where } j \neq i\text{).}$$

Every machine induces a strategy (in the "rule of behavior" sense). Of course, any strategy can be executed by a machine with an infinite number of states (each representing one history of the repeated game). But not every strategy in a repeated game can be executed by a finite machine. For example, consider player 1's strategy to play C, then D, followed by C and twice D, followed by C and thrice D, and so on, independently of player 2's behavior. It is easy to see that this strategy cannot be carried out by a machine with a *finite* number of states.

We are now ready to discuss a new game in which the set of repeated game strategies is replaced with a set of machines. We refer to this game as a *machine game*. The machine game is a two-player strategic game in which each player chooses a (finite) machine to play the infinitely repeated game. The set of strategies for player i in the machine game is the set of all finite machines for player i, denoted by M_i. The players' preferences are taken to be those that are induced from the original repeated game: that is, player i prefers the pair of machines (M_i, M_j) to (M_i', M_j') if in the repeated game, he prefers the sequence of outcomes $(a^t(M_1, M_2))_{t=1,2...}$ to the sequence of outcomes $(a^t(M_1', M_2'))_{t=1,2,...}$. Denote by $U_i(M_1, M_2)$ the repeated game payoff of player i if the players use the machines M_1 and M_2.

By moving from strategies to machines, the only change we have made is that we have restricted the set of strategies to those that can be executed by finite machines. Before moving on to our main objective, that of embedding the complexity of strategies within the model, let us verify that we did not influence the Folk Theorem by limiting the set of strategies.

First, let us demonstrate that whatever player j's machine is, player i can design a machine such that the induced sequence of payoffs is at least as good as the constant sequence of the minmax level, v_j. Let $M_j = (Q, q^*, f, \tau)$ be a machine for player j. The following machine, M_i, chooses player i's best response to the action taken by player j's machine in every period. It does so by "following the moves of player j's machine" and responding with the *myopic* best response. Formally, choose M_i such that the set of states is Q and the initial state is q^*, the same as those of the machine M_j. Define $f_i(q)$ to be i's best response to j's action $f_j(q)$ in the one-shot game G. From q, player i's machine *always* moves to $\tau(q, f_i(q))$. Thus, any equilibrium of the repeated game with either limit of means or a discounting criterion must yield a payoff vector that is enforceable. Note that M_i is not necessarily the best response to M_j in the sense of a machine game, that is, with regard to the repeated game preferences.

The following is the basic Folk Theorem stated for the limit of means criterion in the machine game.

Proposition 8.3 Let w be an enforceable feasible payoff profile of G. A Nash equilibrium of the machine game with the limit of means exists that induces w as a payoff vector.

Proof There is a sequence of outcomes $a^1, \ldots, a^K$, so that $w = \Sigma_{k=1,\ldots,K} u(a^k)/K$. We construct an equilibrium consisting of a pair of "grim" strategies. The machine for player i is:

- *The set of states* $\{Norm^1, \ldots, Norm^K, p\}$.
- *The initial state* $Norm^1$.

- *The output function*   At the state $Norm^k$, play a_i^k. At the state p, play σ_{-j} (a maxmin strategy against player j).
- *Transition*   From state $Norm^k$, if the opponent played a_j^k (which he was meant to play) move to $Norm^{k+1(mod\ K)}$; otherwise move to p.

Thus, the machine for player i plays the "master plan" until player j deviates in which case player i forever chooses σ_{-j}. Since w is enforceable this constitutes an equilibrium. □

The analogous result holds for the discounting case. Thus the restriction of the set of strategies to those implemented by machines (with finite number of states) does not affect the content of the Folk Theorem.

To summarize, we briefly described the "Folk Theorems," theorems that, under a variety of assumptions concerning the players' preferences, establish that a large set of payoff vectors can be obtained by Nash (and even subgame perfect) equilibria in an infinitely repeated game with the limit of means or when δ is large enough. A proof of a Folk Theorem entails the construction of some equilibria that generate the required outcomes but without any requirements being imposed on either the complexity or the soundness of the strategies involved.

We are now ready to proceed toward our main objective in this chapter: the analysis of the repeated game model in which players take into account the complexity of the strategies they employ.

8.4 Complexity Considerations in Repeated Games

We have seen that the restriction that strategies be implementable by machines does not alter the Folk Theorem. If, however, we assume that each player values both his payoff in the repeated game and the simplicity of his strategy, then we obtain results that are very different from the Folk Theorem.

We first have to define what we mean by the complexity of a strategy. We adopt a naive approach: The *complexity*, $c(M)$, of the machine $M = (Q, q^0, f, \tau)$ is taken to be its number of states (the cardinality of Q). The analysis is sensitive to the measure of complexity that is used. This should be considered a *merit* of the model. The measure of complexity is an additional piece of information concerning the strategic reasoning involved in the situation, and should reflect the relevant difficulties of the player in carrying out a strategy. It seems intuitive that different complexity considerations may have different effects in different circumstances.

We began the chapter with the one-shot game G and the repeated game. We then analyzed the machine game with no complexity considerations. We have now reached the final destination of this chapter: a machine game *with* complexity considerations. This game is almost identical to the machine game without complexity considerations. Each of the two players simultaneously chooses a machine. A player's preferences are positively sensitive to his payoff in the repeated game played by the machines. The new feature is that a player's preferences are also negatively sensitive to the complexity of the machine.

Definition A *machine game* of an infinitely repeated game of $G = (N, \{A_i\}, \{u_i\})$ with the complexity measure $c(M)$, is a strategic game with the set of players N, in which for each player i:

• The set of strategies is M_i, the set of all finite machines for player i in the infinitely repeated game.

• Each player i's preferences over the pairs of machines, $\succsim_i$, is increasing with player i's payoff in the repeated game and is decreasing with the complexity of his machine. In other words, $(M_1, M_2) \succ_i (M_1', M_2')$ whenever either $U_i(M_1, M_2) > U_i(M_1', M_2')$ and $c(M_i) = c(M_i')$ or, $U_i(M_1', M_2') = U_i(M_1', M_2')$ and $c(M_i) < c(M_i')$.

In one special case each player's preferences are represented by the function $U_i(M_1, M_2) - \gamma c(M_i)$ with some $\gamma > 0$, interpreted as the cost of each state of the machine. Another special case is one in which the preferences are *lexicographic,* such that each player is concerned first with his payoff in the repeated game and second with the complexity of his machine. This case is especially interesting because lexicographic preferences are those closest to the preferences in the standard model of a repeated game in which complexity considerations are absent. We shall see that even in this case, the set of Nash equilibria payoff vectors is dramatically smaller than the set of all enforceable payoff vectors.

Suppose that the game G is the Prisoner's Dilemma, and consider the two-state machine M that implements the "grim" strategy of Example 1. If the players' common discount factor δ is not too small, then, in the δ-discounted repeated game of G, this machine is a best response to the other player using M. Even by using a more complex machine, player 1 cannot achieve a higher payoff in the repeated game. However, although there is no machine that yields player 1 a higher payoff in the repeated game than does M, given that player 2 uses M, there *is* a machine with one state in which C is played, and it yields player 1 the *same* payoff and is less complex. The state q_D in the machine M is designed to allow a player to threaten his opponent but, in equilibrium, this threat is redundant since each player always chooses C. Thus, either player can drop the state q_D without affecting the outcome; hence, (M, M) is not a Nash equilibrium of the machine game.

On the other hand, consider the following machine, M, presented in figure 8.4. The behavior this machine generates can be interpreted as beginning with a display of the ability to punish. Following this display, the player begins a cooperative phase in which he plays C, threatening to punish a deviant by moving back to the initial state. If both players use this machine, then the sequence of payoffs in the repeated game is 1 followed by an infinite sequence of 3's.

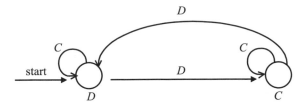

Figure 8.4

If the players' common discount factor δ is not too small, then
(M, M) is a Nash equilibrium of the machine game if the players'
preferences give relatively low weight to complexity (as is the case
if their preferences are either lexicographic or additive with a small
cost of complexity). The argument goes as follows. To increase his
payoff in the repeated game, a player must sometimes choose D
when his opponent plays C. Any such choice of D causes the other
machine to choose D for at least one period, so that when δ is close
enough to 1, a player does not gain by such a maneuver (4 + δ < 3
+ 3δ for δ > 1/2). Thus, for a large enough δ, a player cannot increase
his payoff in the repeated game with any machine, however complex. It is clear that a player in the repeated game cannot achieve
the same payoff by using a less complex machine.

8.5 The Structure of Machine Game Equilibria

In this section, we will restrict our attention, for simplicity's sake,
to an infinitely repeated game in which the players' preferences are
represented by the discounting criterion. We will study the players'
behavior in a two-player δ-discounted infinitely repeated game.

Our aim is to characterize the properties of the structure of
machine game Nash equilibria. In what follows, (M_1^*, M_2^*) is an
equilibrium of the machine game. The analysis is divided into three
stages.

Stage 1 **The number of states in the two machines is equal and the equilibrium of the machine game is an equilibrium of the repeated game.**

First, note that in equilibrium, all states are used at least once: For every state q_i of the machine M_i^*, there exists a period t such that $q_i^t(M_1^*, M_2^*) = q_i$. Otherwise, player i can omit the state q_i, thereby reducing the complexity but not reducing the repeated game's payoff.

Second, let us now turn to a somewhat technical but important observation. For any strategy s_j of player j in the repeated game, denote by $U_j(M_i^*, s_j)$, player j's payoff in the repeated game when he uses a strategy s_j and player i uses the strategy that corresponds to M_i^*. Since M_i^* is finite, player j's problem $\max_{s_j} U_j(M_i^*, s_j)$ of finding a best response (ignoring complexity) to the machine M_i^* in the repeated game has a solution (see Derman [1970, Theorem 1, p. 23]). We are also capable of characterizing the response in the following way: Having $M_i^* = (Q_i, q_i^0, f_i, \tau_i)$, for each $q \in Q_i$, let $V_j(q) = \max_{s_j} U_j(M_i^*(q), s_j)$, where $M_i^*(q)$ is the machine that differs from M_i^* only in the initial state, q. For each $q \in Q_i$, let $A_j(q)$ be the set of solutions to the problem:

$$\max_{a_j \in A_j} u_j(f_i(q), a_j) + \delta V_j(\tau_i(q, a_j)).$$

Player j's strategy is a best response, in the repeated game, to the strategy which corresponds to M_i^* if and only if the action he takes when player i's machine is in state q is a member of $A_j(q)$.

Consider now the problem $\max_{M_j} U_j(M_i^*, M_j)$. This problem differs from $\max_{s_j} U_j(M_i^*, s_j)$ only in that instead of choosing a strategy, player j has to choose a machine. However, even in the restricted scope of the optimization, player j can obtain $\max_{s_j} U_j(M_i^*, s_j)$, by the machine in which the set of states and the initial state are the same as in M_i^*, the output function f_j is defined by $f_j(q) = a_j^*(q) \in A_j(q)$, and the transition function τ_j is defined by $\tau_j(q, x) = \tau_i(q, f_j(q))$ for any $x \in A_i$.

This machine carries out a strategy that is optimal from among all strategies (and thus also solves the problem $\max_{M_j} U_j(M_i^*, M_j)$). Note that the number of states used by this machine is not higher than the number of states in M_i^*.

We are now able to conclude stage 1 of the analysis.

Proposition 8.4 If (M_1^*, M_2^*) is a Nash equilibrium of a machine game, then $c(M_1^*) = c(M_2^*)$ and the pair of strategies in the repeated game associated with (M_1^*, M_2^*) is a Nash equilibrium of the repeated game.

Proof For every i, the solution to the problem $\max_{M_j} U_j(M_i^*, M_j)$ (the problem in which the complexity element is ignored) does not involve more than $c(M_i^*)$ states. Therefore, it must be that in equilibrium (where the complexity element is not ignored) $c(M_j^*) \le c(M_i^*)$. Hence, $c(M_1^*) = c(M_2^*)$. Further, because player j can use a machine with $c(M_i^*)$ states to achieve a payoff in the repeated game equal to $\max_{s_f} U_j(M_i^*, s_j)$, it follows that each of the machines corresponds to a best response strategy in the repeated game. $\square$

Stage 2 **The One-to-One Correspondence Between Actions on the Equilibrium Path**

We will now derive a result that has strong implications on the set of Nash equilibria of a machine game. To obtain some intuition of this result, consider the pair of machines for the infinitely repeated Prisoner's Dilemma shown in figure 8.5.

This pair of machines generates a path in which there are initially $k \ge 2$ periods with the outcome (D, D) (the players display their threats), followed by a cycle of length four with the outcomes (C, C), (C, C), (C, D) and (D, C), which is repeated indefinitely. Any deviation by a player from the prescribed behavior in the cycle causes his opponent's machine to go to its initial state, thereby punishing the deviant for k periods. The reader can confirm that the pair of machines is a Nash equilibrium of the repeated game when the discount factor δ is close enough to 1. However, the machines do

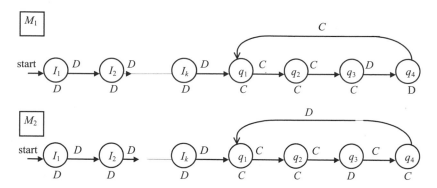

Note: All missing transition arrows are to I_1

Figure 8.5

not constitute an equilibrium of the machine game. To see this, consider M_1 above. In each of the three states, q_1, q_2, and q_3, player 1 takes the same action; he needs the three states in order to "know" when to choose the action D. However, he could adopt the machine M_1', in which the three states, q_1, q_2, and q_3, are replaced by a single state q, in which he chooses C. If M_1' reaches q, it stays there so long as player 2 chooses C and switches to q_4 if player 2 chooses D. The transitions from the state I_k, if player 2 plays D, and from q_4, if player 2 plays C, are corrected to q. Then, (M_1', M_2) generates the same sequence of G-outcomes as does (M_1, M_2); thus, in the machine game, player 1 can profitably deviate to M_1'.

The situation is similar to that in which one paratrooper has to jump after counting to 100 while another has to jump after counting to 101. If the second paratrooper counts, then he can monitor the first paratrooper and make sure he jumps on time. However, counting is costly in the tense environment of the plane, and the second paratrooper can avoid the burden of counting by simply watching his friend and jumping immediately after him.

In general, we can show that if a Nash equilibrium pair of machines generates outcomes in which one of the players takes the same action in two different periods, then the other player takes the same action in those two periods (contrary to the behavior of the players in periods $k + 2$ and $k + 3$ of the example we have just discussed). We can now complete stage 2 of the analysis.

Proposition 8.5 If (M_1^*, M_2^*) is a Nash equilibrium of a machine game, then there is a one-to-one correspondence between the actions of player 1 and player 2, prescribed by M_1^* *and* M_2^*: that is, if $a_i^t(M_1^*, M_2^*) = a_i^s(M_1^*, M_2^*)$ for some $t \neq s$, then $a_j^t(M_1^*, M_2^*) = a_j^s(M_1^*, M_2^*)$.

Proof Let $M_i^* = (Q_i, q_i^0, f_i, \tau_i)$. By proposition 8.4, M_j^* is a best response to M_i^* in the repeated game sense; therefore $f_j(q_j^t(M_1^*, M_2^*)) \in A_j(q_i^t(M_1^*, M_2^*))$ for all t. Thus, if there are two periods t and s in which

$a_j^t(M_1^*, M_2^*) = a_j^s(M_1^*, M_2^*)$ and $a_i^t(M_1^*, M_2^*) \neq a_i^s(M_1^*, M_2^*)$, then

$q_i^t(M_1^*, M_2^*) \neq q_i^s(M_1^*, M_2^*)$,

$f_j(q_i^t(M_1^*, M_2^*)) \in A_j(q_i^t(M_1^*, M_2^*))$ and

$f_j(q_i^s(M_1^*, M_2^*)) \in A_j(q_i^s(M_1^*, M_2^*))$.

We have seen that in equilibrium, $c(M_i^*) = c(M_j^*)$; however, the following describes a machine which carries out an optimal strategy for player j using only $c(M_i^*) - 1$ states.

- The set of states is $Q_i - \{q_i^s\}$.
- The initial state is q_i^0 if $q_i^s \neq q_i^0$ and is q_i^t otherwise.
- The output function is defined by f_j.
- The transition function is defined as follows:

$$\tau_j(q, x0) = \left\{ \begin{array}{ll} \tau_i'(q, f_j(q)) & \text{if } q \neq q_i^t \text{ and} \\ \tau_i'(q_i^s, f_j(q_i^s)) & \text{if } q = q_i^t \text{ and } x = a_i^s(M_1^*, M_2^*) \\ \tau_i'(q_i^t, f_j(q_i^t)) & \text{if } q \neq q_i^t \text{ and } x \neq a_i^s(M_1^*, M_2^*) \end{array} \right.$$

where τ_i' is identical to τ_i except that $\tau_i'(q, x) = q_i^t$ whenever $\tau_i(q, x) = q_i^s$. $\square$

This result has a striking implication for the equilibrium outcome path where G is a 2×2 game. For example, when G is the Prisoner's Dilemma, the G-outcomes played in equilibrium must be either in the set $\{(C, C), (D, D)\}$ or in the set $\{(C, D), (D, C)\}$.

Stage 3 The One-to-One Correspondence Between States on the Equilibrium Path

We now turn to the structure of the equilibrium machines. Because each player's machine is finite, there is a minimal number t' such that for some $t > t'$, we have $q_i^t = q_i^{t'}$ for *both* i. Let t^* be the minimal period t, such that $t > t'$ and $q_i^t = q_i^{t'}$ for both i. The sequence of pairs of states starting in period t' is a cycle of length $t^* - t'$. We refer to this stage as the *cycling phase* and to the stage before period t' as the *introductory phase*.

We now show that the sets of states a player uses in the cycling and introductory phases are disjoint. Furthermore, in the introductory phase, each state is "visited" only once and each of a player's cycle states are repeated only once in each cycle. Thus, in equilibrium, there is a one-to-one correspondence between the states in the machines of players 1 and 2. This means that in every period each machine "knows" the state of the other machine.

Proposition 8.6 If (M_1^*, M_2^*) is an equilibrium of a machine game, then there exists a period t^* and an integer $\ell < t^*$ such that for $i = 1, 2$, the states in the sequence $(q_i^t(M_1^*, M_2^*))_{t=1,2,\ldots,t^*-1}$ are distinct and $q_i^t(M_1^*, M_2^*) = q_i^{t-\ell}(M_1^*, M_2^*)$ for $t \geq t^*$.

Proof Let t^* be the first period in which one of the states of either of the two machines appears for the second time. That is, let t^* be the minimal time for which there is a player i and a period $t_i < t^*$ such that $q_i^{t^*} = q_i^{t_i}$ have $a_i^{t^*} = a_i^{t_i}$; hence, by the previous stage $a_j^{t^*} = a_j^{t_i}$ It follows that for all $k \geq 0$ we have $q_i^{t^*+k} = q_i^{t_i+k}$; because in equilibrium all states appear at least once, we find that $C(M_i^*) = t^* - 1$. By the definition of t^*, it follows that all states of M_j^* through time $t^* - 1$ are distinct, and because in equilibrium $C(M_j^*) = C(M_i^*)$, there exists $t_j < t^*$ such that $q_j^{t_j} = q_j^{t^*}$. It remains to show that $t_j = t_i$. Assume to the contrary that, say, $t_j > t_i$. Then player j can obtain the same path of outcomes with a machine in which $q_j^{t_i}$ is excluded by making a transition from $q_j^{t_i - 1}$ to $q_j^{t^*}$, omitting $q_j^{t_i}$. Because this machine has the property that whenever the machine M_i^* is at a state q, player j plays an action in $A_j(q)$, an optimal repeated game strategy is induced using a machine with fewer states than M_j^*, contradicting that (M_1^*, M_2^*) is an equilibrium. □

Comment The results in this section show that the set of equilibria of the machine game is much smaller than that of the repeated game. Of course, to characterize the exact set of equilibria would depend on the exact preference relations. Consider, for example, the repeated Prisoner's Dilemma and the case in which the two players' preferences in the machine game are lexicographic. We already know that either a subset of $\{(C, C), (D, D)\}$ or a subset of $\{(C, D), (D, C)\}$ can be realized on an equilibrium path. One can show that for any two non-negative integers, n_C and n_D, for δ high enough there exists an equilibrium with a cycle of length $n_C + n_D$ in which (C, C) appears n_C times and (D, D) appears n_D times (Project 2).

In order to construct equilibria in which every outcome on the equilibrium path is either (C, D) or (D, C), one does not require an introductory phase. For all positive integers n_1 and n_2 satisfying $4n_i/(n_1 + n_2) > 1$ for both i and large enough δ, there is an equilibrium of the machine game in which the cycle starts immediately and consists of n_1 plays of (D, C) followed by n_2 plays of (C, D) without any introductory phase. (The condition on n_1 and n_2 ensures that each player's average payoff exceeds his minmax payoff of 1.)

An equilibrium for the case $n_1 = n_2 = 1$ is shown in figure 8.6. One interpretation of this equilibrium is that the players alternate at being generous toward each other. One can think of (C, D) as the

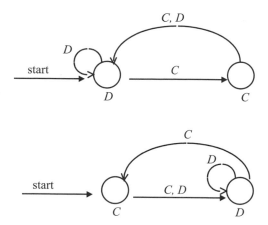

Figure 8.6

event in which player 1 gives a gift to player 2 and (D, C) as the event in which player 2 gives a gift to player 1. In equilibrium, a player does not care if his opponent refuses the gift (i.e., chooses C when he could have chosen D and receive the gift), but he insists that his opponent give him a gift (play C) in periods in which he expects to receive one. If he does not receive a gift, then he does not move to the state in which he is generous.

8.6 Repeated Extensive Games

The analysis in the previous sections was confined to the analysis of the model of the repeated game in which the one-shot game is a strategic one. This type of analysis could, in principle, be applied to other families of games. One example, discussed briefly here, is an infinitely repeated game in which the one-shot game is an extensive game. Although the analysis of the Nash equilibria of the (regular) repeated extensive game is identical to that of the repeated game of the corresponding strategic form game (though the set of subgame perfect equilibria may sometimes be different), the analysis of the Nash equilibria of the *machine* game of the extensive game

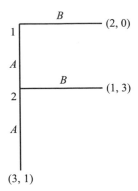

Figure 8.7

raises a new issue regarding the interpretation of the repeated game of an extensive game. Consider, for example, the repeated game of the extensive game Γ (fig. 8.7). The normal form of Γ is the game G:

	A	B
A	3, 1	1, 3
B	2, 0	2, 0

Applying the previous section's analysis to the game G, it is easy to verify that any path of a Nash equilibrium of the corresponding machine game contains only the outcomes (A, A) and (B, B) (any path on the auxiliary diagonal yields a payoff less than what player 1 can guarantee by constantly playing B). If the players' preferences in the machine game are lexicographic, then every finite sequence containing only the outcomes (A, A) and (B, B) is, for large enough δ, a cycling phase of a path associated with some Nash equilibrium of the machine game.

The analysis of the repeated game of Γ requires an additional specification. What does player 1 know at the end of each round? It seems reasonable to assume that the players are only informed of the terminal history of that period's play. That is, if player 1 chooses B, he has no knowledge of player 2's plan were he to have played A.

In the machine game we are now analyzing, a machine's output is a Γ-strategy and an input is a Γ-outcome. It is easy to verify that our previous arguments apply here and that there is no equilibrium of the machine game such that the players sometimes play (A, A) and sometimes (A, B); that is, in any equilibrium, the path of Γ-outcomes must be a string of (A, A)'s and (B, B)'s only. However, further investigation shows that there is no equilibrium path in which (A, A) appears. If there were, then player 2 could make do with a one-state machine that always plays A. Then, it must be that player 1 is using the one-state machine that plays A; but if so, player 2 can deviate profitably to the one-state machine that plays B, a contradiction. Thus, the only equilibrium of the machine game involves player 1 using the one-state machine that plays B, while player 2 uses the one-state machine that "threatens" to play B.

We see that the machine game equilibrium is sensitive to details regarding information and ability to monitor. The machine game attached to the strategic game G represents a situation in which observing the opponent's plans is possible and costless. In the machine game attached to the extensive game Γ, a player cannot observe the opponent's plans unless they are realized. No wonder that in a model like the machine game, in which the costs of having plans as well as acquiring and processing information are important components in the players' considerations, the difference between these two machine games can be significant.

8.7 Concluding Remarks

The Model and Bounded Rationality

The analysis in this chapter has revealed once again a fundamental tension that exists when "modeling bounded rationality." In a machine game, a player has to solve a maximization problem in which he balances two desires: achieving a high payoff versus employing a simple machine. In some sense, this problem is more complicated than that of finding an optimal strategy in the conventional repeated game, since the player must also consider the complexity of his rule of behavior, not just the payoff. Although the model imposes restrictions on the ability of the players to implement their repeated game strategy, it does not impose any constraint on the player's ability to solve his optimality problem in the machine game.

I do not find this fact to be peculiar. The tradeoff between complexity and optimality is very common in real life. Often, a decision maker may make very complicated computations regarding his "lower level agents" (probably his own selves) while taking into account the limitations on those agents' ability to implement their instructions.

Dynamic Considerations

A machine game is a one-shot game in which a player cannot alter his machine in the course of implementing the strategy.

The model would be quite uninteresting if we allowed the players to freely alter their machine every period; they would need only a single state machine each period, and the repeated game consideration would be pushed from the machine level to the level of the strategy determining the change of machines in that state.

A more attractive possibility would be to integrate dynamic considerations into the model by requiring that after every history of the repeated game, the pair of machines be an equilibrium of the machine game. This requirement implies that the equilibrium play of the machines is such that any state in any machine must be used infinitely often. In particular, it would mean the absence of an introductory phase. This requirement may have a strong additional effect on the set of equilibria. For example, in the infinitely repeated Prisoner's Dilemma, every equilibrium in which (C, C) is one of the outcomes must have an introductory phase (Project 4), and thus any equilibrium in which all states are used infinitely often, induces either a constant play of (D, D) or a play of (C, D)'s and (D, C)'s exclusively.

8.8 Bibliographic Notes

Most of this chapter is based on Rubinstein (1986) and Abreu and Rubinstein (1988).

For a more detailed discussion and references regarding the basic results of the model of repeated games with perfect information, see Chapter 8 of Osborne and Rubinstein (1994). For a discussion of the notion of automatae, see Hopcroft and Ullman (1979).

The arguments in Section 4 are a modification of the original proof of Abreu and Rubinstein (1988), developed in Piccione (1992). Section 6 is based on Piccione and Rubinstein (1993).

8.9 Projects

1. *Exercise* (From Osborne and Rubinstein [1994].) Give an example of a three-player game for which the associated machine game has a Nash equilibrium in which it is not true that all three machines have the same number of states.

2. *Exercise* (From Abreu and Rubinstein [1988].) Show that for every N_C and N_D and for every δ close enough to 1, there is an equilibrium for the machine game (with G being the Prisoner's Dilemma) so that in the equilibrium path cycle, the players play N_D times (D, D) and N_C times (C, C) with an introductory phase in which they play (D, D). Why is the order of play in the cycle important?

3. *Exercise* (From Piccione [1992].) Explain in what sense the analysis of the machine game is sensitive to "duplicating action" in the one-shot game. Does it make sense?

4. *Exercise* (From Rubinstein [1986].) Show that in the infinitely repeated Prisoner's Dilemma, every equilibrium of the machine game in which (C, C) is one of the outcomes must have an introductory phase.

5. *Reading* (From Neme and Quintas [1990].) Consider the machine game discussed in this chapter with the limit of means and the one modification that each player can use an *infinite* number of states (yet is interested to reduce the number of states). Show that any enforceable payoff vector can be supported in equilibrium.

6. *Exercise* (From Banks and Sundaram [1990].) Study a modification of the model in which monitoring the other player's behavior is also costly. More precisely, assume that a player cares about three numbers in lexicographic order: (1) his repeated game payoff, (2) the number of states in his machine, and (3) the number of transition arrows in his machine. Show that the set of Nash equilibrium paths for this model includes only strings of one-shot Nash equilibria. Go through the following steps.

In any equilibrium:

1. The number of *transitions* in a player's machine has to be at least as large as the number of *states* in his machine (otherwise, some states are unreachable).

2. The number of states of the two machines is equal.

3. The number of transitions in each machine is equal to the number of states.

4. In the play of the equilibrium, machine i goes through all its states and then returns to the state that was used at period k_i. Show that $k_1 = k_2$.

5. Player i's action at each state must be a best response to the corresponding player j's action.

7. *Innovative* Suggest an interesting economic model in which each economic agent takes into account both his "conventional utility" and the complexity of his strategy. You may consult Chatterjee and Sabourian (1996), who analyze the multiperson bargaining game.

9

Attempts to Resolve the Finite Horizon Paradoxes

9.1 Motivation

An issue constantly discussed in game theory is that of the "finite horizon paradoxes." The most noticeable examples are the finitely repeated Prisoner's Dilemma, Rosenthal's centipede game, and Selten's chain store paradox. In these games, the standard game-theoretic solutions yield results that are considered quite unintuitive. This fact has prompted game theorists to consider the appropriateness of the basic solution concepts. It has also motivated another approach, discussed in this chapter, which tries to explain the unintuitive results by the players' lack of full rationality.

For concreteness, we will focus on a timing game that is simpler in some respects than the games mentioned above and yet has the features we need for our discussion. The game is similar to the finitely repeated Prisoner's Dilemma; its one divergent feature being that as soon as at least one of the players does not cooperate, the game is over.

Let $G_0(T)$ be an extensive game with two players, 1 and 2. The game takes place at T periods enumerated 1, 2, . . . , T. In each period, the two players have to choose simultaneously whether to stop the game or allow it to continue; that is, each player has two alternatives in every period, Stop or Continue (Cont). The game continues from period t to period $t + 1$ only if *both* players choose

Cont. Each player accumulates payoffs during the course of the game. At the end of any period (including period T) in which both players choose Cont, each player adds 3 to his payoff. If both choose Stop, each receives 1. If one of them chooses Stop and the other chooses Cont, the player who stops the game receives 5 while the other receives 0. The important feature of these payoffs is that it is optimal for player i to stop the game at period t if and only if he believes that player j intends to stop the game at period t or at period $t + 1$. If player i believes that player j will never choose Stop, then player i will do best by stopping the game at period T.

The set of nonterminal histories consists of all sequences of t mutual choices of Cont for $0 \leq t < T$. A player's strategy (plan of action) specifies the period in which the player plans to stop the game, if at all. Thus, a player in $G_0(T)$ has T strategies, $S(1), \ldots,$ $S(T)$, where $S(t)$ is "stop at period t," and one strategy of "never stop," denoted by CONT. Note that the conventional game-theoretical notion of strategy is somewhat different, but the current notion of a strategy is appropriate here; see Section 8.3 and Rubinstein (1991) for discussion of this point.

In spite of the potential "enormous gains" the players can obtain if they continue the game to its "happy end," the game has only one Nash equilibrium outcome, in which both players stop the game at the first period. It is not difficult to verify that the game does not have any additional mixed-strategy equilibria.

The rest of the chapter is devoted to a review of several approaches that attempt to resolve the finite horizon paradoxes. Do these approaches provide a satisfactory resolution of the paradoxical aspects that appear in $G_0(T)$?

9.2 Implementation of Strategies by Machines

The computation necessary to execute the strategy $S(t)$ for $t > 1$ involves counting up to t. The implementation of the strategies CONT and $S(1)$ does not require any computation. Thus, the possibilities to model complexity of strategies are quite limited. The only possible complexity issue concerns the difficulty of a player in identifying his planned stopping time. Other complexity issues that appeared in Chapter 8 are not relevant to $G_0(T)$. A player cannot monitor his opponent, because if he chooses Stop, the game is over. Players have no possibility of reaching a long-term compromise based on diversifying their actions along the time dimension in that there is only one action that does not end the game. A history (information about past events) is fully described by its length.

Readers may wonder whether the difficulties in counting can be a reasonable basis for a serious model. I think that there are contexts in which it is reasonable to assume that the larger the t, the more complex it is to count up to t (have you ever received an instruction to turn right at the seventeenth intersection?). In any case, one should not take the analysis too literally as its main purpose is to demonstrate the logic of complexity considerations in interactive situations.

As in Chapter 8, we describe the complexity of a strategy by the minimal number of states in the machine that implements the strategy. A machine here is a finite automaton that receives as input the signal "one period has passed" and generates as output one action Cont or Stop. That is, a machine is a four-tuple (Q, q_0, f, τ) where Q is a finite set of states, $q_0 \in Q$ is the initial state, the output function $f: Q \rightarrow \{Stop, Cont\}$ specifies an action Stop or Cont for every state, and $\tau: Q \rightarrow Q$ is a transition function.

Note that in Chapter 8, an automaton's transition function determined how the machine moved from one state to another in response to the input it received. Here, as long as the game continues, there is only one possible input (Cont); thus, we can write the transition function as a function from Q into Q.

Of course, any strategy in $G_0(T)$ is implementable by a machine. There exists a machine, $M(t)$, with t states (but no less), that carries out the strategy $S(t)$. The strategy CONT is implementable by a one-state machine, $M(CONT)$.

The three machine games described in the next three sections are variants of $G_0(T)$. In all these games, a player makes a strategic decision only once, before the game starts, and chooses a machine that implements his strategy and operates automatically with no further deliberation on his part. In the first game, we modify the payoff functions to incorporate the complexity costs; in the second game, we put a bound on the complexity of the feasible machines; in the third, we further modify the notion of a machine so that besides playing the game $G_0(T)$, it has to send as well as receive messages.

9.3 Counting is Costly

In this section, we apply the approach in which complexity is costly. Each player wishes to increase his $G_0(T)$ payoff and to decrease the complexity of his machine. Let $c > 0$. In the machine game $G_1(T, c)$, each player has to choose a machine and a player's utility is [payoff in $G_0(T)$] $- c \times$ [the number of states].

Proposition 9.1 If $c \geq 2/(T - 1)$, then the pairs of machines $(M(CONT), M(CONT))$ and $(M(1), M(1))$ are the only (pure) equilibria of $G_1(T, c)$. If $c < 2/(T - 1)$, then the pair of machines $(M(1), M(1))$ is the only equilibrium of $G_1(T, c)$.

Proof First, note that in equilibrium, if one of the players uses the machine $M(1)$, the other uses the machine $M(1)$. Thus, the pair $(M(1), M(1))$ is always an equilibrium of $G_1(T, c)$. Note also that if in equilibrium one player uses $M(CONT)$, then the other does not use any $M(t)$ with $t < T$ because deviating to $M(CONT)$ increases his payoff in $G_0(T)$ and decreases the complexity of his machine.

There is no equilibrium in which one of the players, let us say player 1, uses $M(t)$ with $1 < t < T$ because the best response of player 2 must be $M(CONT)$, $M(1)$ or some $M(t')$ with $t' < t$. We have seen that $(M(t), M(\text{CONT}))$ $(t < T)$ and $(M(t), M(1))$ $(t > 1)$ are not equilibria. The pair $(M(t), M(t'))$ with $1 < t' \leq t$ is not an equilibrium because player 1 can profitably deviate to $M(t' - 1)$ with fewer states and higher payoff.

The pair $(M(T), M(\text{CONT}))$ also is not an equilibrium. Either $c > 2/(T - 1)$ or $2/(T - 2) > c$. If $c > 2/(T - 1)$, player 1 will do better by deviating to $M(\text{CONT})$, losing 2 from his payoff in $G_0(T)$ and saving $T - 1$ states. If $2/(T - 2) > c$, player 2 can profit by switching to the machine $M(T - 1)$, using $T - 2$ more states, but gaining 2 units of payoff.

Finally, $(M(\text{CONT}), M(\text{CONT}))$ is an equilibrium only if it is not worthwhile for a player to deviate to $M(T)$, namely, if $c \geq 2/(T - 1)$. $\square$

Remark In Chapter 8, adding complexity costs to the players' considerations reduced the set of equilibrium outcomes. In contrast, the set of Nash equilibrium outcomes of $G_1(T, c)$ is not necessarily a subset of the set of Nash equilibria of $G_0(T)$; when c is large, we have a new equilibrium outcome in which the game continues to the end.

9.4 Bounded Capability to Count

In this section, we modify the game $G_0(T)$ so that players will be restricted in the complexity of strategy they can employ. Let B be a natural number. In the game $G_2(T, B)$, each of the players has to choose (simultaneously) a machine that plays the game $G_0(T)$, having no more than B states. The payoffs are as in the game $G_0(T)$. Unlike in $G_1(T, c)$, the use of the B states is free; however, the players cannot use a machine with more than B states.

The analysis of $G_2(T, B)$ is trivial. If $B < T$, that is, if the players are unable to count up to T, then the "good cooperative outcome" can emerge in equilibrium; but if they are able to count up to T $(B \geq T)$, then the existence of a restriction on the number of states does not produce any new equilibrium outcomes.

Proposition 9.2 *In* $G_2(T, B)$:

1. If $B \geq T$, then the only Nash equilibrium is $(M(1), M(1))$.

2. If $B < T$, then both $(M(\text{CONT}), M(\text{CONT}))$ and $(M(1), M(1))$ are the only pure Nash equilibria of the game.

Proof (1) If $B \geq T$, then the machine game $G_2(T, B)$ is identical to $G_0(T)$ because all strategies of $G_0(T)$ can be implemented by machines with not more than T states. (2) A machine that, when playing against $M(\text{CONT})$, yields a $G_0(T)$-payoff higher than does $M(\text{CONT})$, has to have T states, which are unavailable when $B < T$. □

9.5 Machines Also Send Messages

In contrast to the game $G_2(T, B)$, the game constructed in this section has a "good equilibrium," whatever the bound on the number of states is. However, in order to achieve this result we will change the meaning of a machine. In this section, a machine, besides playing the game $G_0(T)$, is involved in sending meaningless messages. In the "good equilibrium" the need to send the right messages diverts available resources (states) from being used to count up to T and thereby prevents a profitable deviation. This is an appealing strategic idea, is a reminder of a real-life common strategic maneuver in which one player diverts the attention of his opponent to prevent that opponent from taking an undesirable action.

Let L be a set of symbols (messages). An action–message machine is a set of states Q, an initial state $q_0 \in Q$, an output function $f: Q \to \{\text{Stop}\} \cup \{(\text{Cont}, m): m \in L\}$, and a transition function $\tau: Q \times L \to Q$. The meaning of $f(q) = (\text{Cont}, m)$ is that at the state q, the machine chooses Cont and sends the message m; $f(q) = \text{Stop}$ means that at q the machine chooses Stop. The meaning of $\tau(q, m) = q'$ is that while at the state q, if the message m is received from the other player, the machine moves to state q'. In the game $G_3(T, B, L)$, a player has to choose an action–message machine using the set of messages L, with no more than B states. Payoffs are as in $G_0(T)$.

Proposition 9.3 For all $T \geq 2$ and for all B (even $B > T!$), there is a set of messages, L, such that the game $G_3(T, B, L)$ has a *mixed* strategy equilibrium with the outcome that no player ever stops the game.

Proof Let $L = L_1 \cup L_2$ where L_i is a set with $B - 2$ elements and L_1 and L_2 are disjoint. Let s_i be player i's mixed strategy, in which he picks, with probability $1/(B - 2)$, a B-state machine that initially sends the message $m^* \in L_i$, and then repeats the message sent by player j; if the machine detects that the other machine does not reply with the message m^*, it stops the game. More precisely the set of states in this machine is $L_j \cup \{m^*, S\}$. The following table describes the output and transaction functions.

	State q	Output $f(q)$	Transition $\tau(q, n)$
(initial)	m^*	(Cont, m^*)	n
	$n^* \varepsilon Lj$	(Cont, n^*)	$\begin{cases} n^* & \text{if } n = m^* \\ S & \text{otherwise} \end{cases}$
	S	Stop.	

It is not difficult to verify that (s_1, s_2) defined above is a mixed strategy equilibrium of $G_3(T, B, L)$. In order for player i to increase his payoff in $G_0(T)$ in the event that player j announces a message m, he must devote $T - 1$ states to the possibility that j will announce m. This means that in order to obtain this "small" gain of 2 with probability $1/(B-2)$, he has to suffer a "big" loss due to his inability to respond appropriately to $T - 1$ other messages (which will be sent with probability $(T - 1)/(B - 2)$). $\square$

Comment on the Finitely Repeated Prisoner's Dilemma
The idea behind G_3 originated in Neyman (1985), which analyzes the finitely repeated Prisoner's Dilemma. Neyman considers a

machine game associated with the T-finitely repeated Prisoner's Dilemma, in which each player can use a machine with no more than $B(T)$ states. If $B(T)$ is polynomial in T and T is large enough, then the game has a mixed strategy equilibrium outcome that is "close" to the cooperative outcome. The strategic idea behind the construction of the equilibrium is similar to that just discussed. In Neyman's game, there are no explicit messages; instead, players use the language of the moves in the game. In the repeated Prisoner's Dilemma (as for any other 2×2 matrix game), one can encode K messages by strings of actions C or D of length $\log_2 K$. The equilibrium starts with a relatively short play in which players use actions to send and confirm messages. Conditional on this phase of communication "going well," the players play cooperatively in (the relatively long) remainder of the game; in case a player does not repeat the message sent to him, then all players switch to playing D repeatedly.

I find it artificial that players use actions as a language to encode messages. In contrast, in $G_3(T, B, L)$ there is no way to encode messages by using actions (any Stop action halts the game); instead, messages are added directly to the game, which allows the "exhausting the ability to count" strategy.

9.6 The ε-Equilibrium Approach: A Deviation Is Costly

Finally, let us discuss another approach, the first attempt to resolve finite horizon paradoxes on the basis of bounded rationality considerations. In this approach, a player who is used to a certain pattern of behavior (equilibrium behavior) needs a "heavyweight" reason to make a change. A good reason to deviate is not just the existence of a positive gain from deviation (as is assumed by the concept of Nash equilibrium), but also the potential gains being above the cost of change. This may reflect the cost of training agents who carry out the strategy, the time it takes for the player to adjust to the change, or the emotional cost required to deviate from convention. According to this approach, players are able to calculate the expected gain from a change and compare it to the cost of change, $\varepsilon > 0$.

This discussion motivates the definition of an *ε-equilibrium* as a pair of strategies (s_1, s_2) such that for any player i, the optimal response to s_j does not yield a payoff that is more than ε higher than the payoff he obtains by using the strategy s_i. Obviously, any Nash equilibrium is also an ε-equilibrium, whatever ε is.

Returning to $G_0(T)$, a small ε ("small" relative to the maximum amount of payoffs that can be accumulated in the game) is sufficient to sustain non-equilibrium modes of behavior. Regardless of the length of the game, no player can gain more than 2 from any deviation from (CONT, CONT). Thus, for any $\varepsilon \geq 2$ and for all T, the pair (CONT, CONT) (as well as many other pairs of strategies) is an ε-equilibrium of $G_0(T)$.

This approach does not provide a persuasive explanation for the exhibited paradoxical behavior. Note that the same ε justifies the ε-equilibrium (CONT, CONT) independently of T. The game $G_0(1)$ is the Prisoner's Dilemma, in which Stop is the dominating strategy. Yet, it is an ε-equilibrium (for $\varepsilon \geq 2$), as for any other game $G_0(T)$.

9.7 Conclusion

In my opinion, none of the approaches presented in this chapter resolves the finite horizon paradoxes. The "resolutions" suggested by G_1 and G_2 can be summarized as follows: If it is too costly or impossible to count up to T (the length of the game), then the paradox "disappears." I disagree with the claims made in some of the literature that a game like G_3 resolves the finite horizon paradoxes. The idea of G_3 is intriguing, but I doubt that the behavior in $G_0(T)$, which is not predicted by the game theoretic equilibrium concept, can be attributed to the players' need to be involved in an activity besides counting. Even in the absence of complexity constraints, even if the players have all the time and talent required to analyze the situation, and even if T is "not large," I doubt that they would stop the game immediately. It seems that the real problem is that whereas a proof by induction is a standard tool in mathematics, it is not part of routine human reasoning. Players in finite horizon games employ different *procedures*. What these procedures are remains, in my opinion, one of the more exciting research tasks.

9.8 Bibliographic Notes

The chapter is based on Rubinstein (1987). The game G_3 follows Neyman (1985); its presentation here is in the spirit of Zemel (1989).

For an introduction to the "finite horizon game paradoxes," see Luce and Raiffa (1957), Rosenthal (1982), and Selten (1978).

The concept of ε-equilibrium was suggested by Radner in the 1970s, and his paper on the subject was finally published in Radner (1986).

9.9 Projects

1. *Innovative* Read Ben-Porath (1993). Find a simpler two-player machine game that will have the property that in equilibrium a player with a larger number of available states does better than the other player.

2. *Reading* Compare the approach in this chapter with the way that Kreps, Milgrom, Roberts, and Wilson (1982) try to resolve the finite horizon paradox.

10 Computability Constraints in Games

10.1 Introduction

This book is devoted to the issue of modeling *bounds* on rationality. The bounds we tried to model in the previous chapters emerge from the fact that rational behavior requires "costly" or "complicated" operations. But, as we know, not every task that can be described in words can be executed by what we perceive to be a computing machine. Thus, one may suspect that even if there were no computational costs, bounds on the ability to pursue the rational man paradigm exist because of fundamental computational "impossibilities." In this chapter, we briefly touch upon this issue.

In order to focus our discussion, consider the Battle of the Sexes:

	a	b
a	2, 1	0, 0
b	0, 0	1, 2

Based merely on the information included in the strategic game, little can be said about the "rational" actions of player 1. Player 1 needs to know how player 2 analyzes the game in order to make any sensible choice. For example, if player 1 knows that player 2 is a "demanding" player who always "goes for the highest payoff," it would be best for player 1 to play *b*. However, if player 1 knows that player 2 is "demanding" only when playing against a "weak" player, the rational action to be taken by player 1 would depend on player 1's beliefs of how player 2 evaluates player 1's character. The idea that a player's rational choice requires knowledge of the *type* of opponent he faces (and not just the preferences of that opponent) is applicable even for games with a unique equilibrium. For example:

	a	b
a	2, 1	0, 0
b	0, 3	1, 2

For player 1 to conclude that he should play *a*, he has to know that player 2 is a player who does not choose a dominated strategy.

The arena in which we will examine the computability constraints is that of a strategic game where each player fully "knows" his opponent. Using game-theoretical terminology, we will refer to the identity of a player as his "type." By this we have in mind a mode of behavior like, "be nice with nice players and aggressive with players who are not nice." We will assume that when a player calculates his choice, the opponent's type is what Binmore (1987) has described as "written on his forehead." This does not mean that the player necessarily uses the entire description of the opponent in his deliberation, but he has access to all the details. On the other hand, we will *not* assume that a player has access to the description of himself. This assumption does not alter the essence of the observations that we will make, but it seems to me that to assume this will be less natural.

What is "a full description of a player" in our context? We certainly want there to be a type t_x who plays x independently of his knowledge of the other player's type. But we also want there to be a type who plays y whenever he sees a type t_x player and plays z in case he meets another type. We quickly realize that the naive definition of a type leads to a huge set. Furthermore, it is impossible to think about a type as if it were just any response function that arbitrarily assigns values to any type he plays against. If it were, the cardinality of the set of types would be the power of its own cardinality, which is of course impossible. Instead, we will think about a type as an algorithm that receives the finite description of the opponent's algorithm as input and produces an action as output.

The assumption that a player knows the other player's type is very strong. Note that this is not the type of "knowledge" we have in equilibrium, where a player "knows" the equilibrium behavior of the other players, probably on the basis of observations of a steady state situation. Here, a player is assumed to recognize the other player's algorithm.

What does it then mean to compute? This issue was a major topic of research in mathematics during the twentieth century. Common to the formal suggestions is the view that a computation is a sequence of simple operations, performed according to some finite set of commands, and using some "working space" (whether on a tape, pieces of paper, and so on) in which memory can be stored during the course of the computation. The operations are of the following type: reading symbols written in one of the sites in the working space, replacing one symbol with another, and moving from one site in the working space to another. The commands instruct the computing device what to do in the working space and how to move from one site to another.

The following is a version of probably the most famous formalization of "computation": the model of a Turing Machine. Imagine a tape consisting of an infinite number of discrete cells with a left end. In each of the cells, one symbol, taken from among a finite set of symbols S, can be written. The input appears, at the start of the machine's operation, on the left side of the tape. The machine works like a finite automaton: It has a finite set of states Q (a subset of the countable set $\{q_0, q_1, q_2 \ldots \}$). The state q_0 is the initial state, and

$F \subseteq Q$ is the set of terminal states of the machine. The transition function of the machine assigns to each pair $(q, s) \in Q \times S$ a triple (q', s', d) where $q' \in Q$ is the next state of the machine, $s' \in S$ is the symbol it writes on the tape cell in place of s, and $d \in \{L, R\}$ is the direction that the head moves on the tape. The machine's operation starts from the initial state, where the machine's head is on the tape's left end. The machine stops as soon as it reaches one of the states in F. Given an input, a machine may not stop. When m is a machine and x is an input, we denote by $m(x)$ the *output* of the m if it stops.

Note that the set of machines is countable. Actually, it is "effectively denumerable" in the sense that we can define an algorithm that will list all possible machines with no repetitions.

Many alternative definitions of computation have been suggested in the literature. A fascinating fact about the different definitions is that all of them have been shown to be equivalent. This is so striking that we feel that this formalization is indeed the "right" one. Church's Thesis states that the formal model of the Turing Machine indeed captures the intuition about what a calculation is. It has led many researchers to believe that every algorithm described in daily language can be translated into any of the suggested formal models. This persuasion is so strong that some authors even find that the formal proofs in this area, which are typically long and tedious, are redundant and that one can make do with verbal proofs. I will abide by that practice, although, I usually believe that "models have to be complete" and that "proofs have to be proofs." Therefore, in the next section, only intuitive arguments are made. For a proper understanding of the material, the reader is urged to consult one of the many excellent books available on the subject.

10.2 Informal Results on Computability

Following are several results that are important for the basic application of computability constraints to the game theoretical setting.

Result 1: The Existence of a Machine That Recognizes Itself

Is there a machine that recognizes itself? We look for a machine m^* that halts with an output say, C, whenever the input is a description of itself and halts with a different output say, D, whenever the input is not m^*. Note the subtlety of the question. The machine cannot simply compare the input with m^* because the description of m^* is not given to m^* as a part of the input. The machine m^* also cannot simply compare the input to a text written within it because the full description of the machine includes more symbols than this text. Thus, we need a more innovative structure. The following algorithm, described plainly, fulfills this task:

Print C and stop if the following fact is true and print D and stop otherwise: the input before and after the third appearance of the word "is" is Print C and stop if the following fact is true and print D and stop otherwise: the input before and after the third appearance of the word "is."

An alternative description of the program:

1. Write this on the tape:
    2. Verify that the other machine has four commands, the last three being identical to the text on the tape.
    3. Check whether command 1 starts with the text "Write this on the tape," followed by the text on the tape.
    4. If the answer to both commands 2 and 3 are positive, print C; otherwise print D.

2. Verify that the other machine has four commands, the last three being identical to the text on the tape.

3. Check whether command 1 starts with the text "Write this text on the tape," followed by the text on the tape.

4. If the answer to both commands 2 and 3 are positive, print C; otherwise print D.

Thus, the circularity can be broken and a machine can recognize itself!

Result 2: The Existence of a Machine That Imitates All Machines

Is there a machine m^* that, whenever it receives as input a pair (m, x), where m is a description of a machine and x is an arbitrary string of symbols, produces the same output that machine m produces if it receives the input x? That is, we are looking for a machine m^* where $m^*(m, x)$ halts iff $m(x)$ halts and, if so, $m^*(m, x) = m(x)$. Note that we do not require that m^* halt with some special symbol when $m(x)$ does not halt.

Such a machine m^* indeed exists, and is called a universal machine. Note that the description of the operation of a machine is algorithmic and can be described by a finite set of instructions to be followed one by one. The basic idea of the construction of a universal machine is that the machine will read the description of m and will use the algorithm that describes its operation to compute its output for the input x.

Result 3: A Machine That Predicts the Outcome of Any Machine Playing Against It

The universal machine m^*, described in Result 2, can calculate, for any m, the output $m(m^*)$ if it gets m^* as input as well. We will now see that a machine exists that can calculate the response of any machine to its own description without getting its own description as an input. That is, we are interested in the construction of a machine m^* that for every machine m will stop if and only if $m(m^*)$ stops and will give the same result as an output. The machine gets m as input. Then it goes through the list of machines (as was mentioned, an effective denumeration of the set of machines exists) until, using the idea of Result 1, it recognizes itself, m^*. Finally it

implements the universal machine, described in Result 2, to produce the output that the input machine, m, produces with the
input m^*.

Result 4: No Machine Predicts Whether a Machine Halts on Receiving It as an Input

The universal machine m, described in Result 3, does not stop at
input m' if $m'(m)$ does not stop. There is no machine m^* that for
every machine m determines whether machine m stops when it
receives the input m^*. To see this assume, by contradiction, that such
an m^* exists. Using the diagonalization idea, construct a machine
m' satisfying that for any input m, it calculates $m^*(m)$; if the output
is "it stops," the machine $m'(m)$ does not stop, and if the output
$m^*(m)$ is "it does not stop," $m'(m)$ does stop. When m' gets as
input m^*, it stops iff m^* predicts that m' does not stop!

Result 5: A Machine That Is Never Correctly Predicted

We are looking for a machine m' that will have the property that
whenever $m(m')$ stops, $m'(m)$ will stop with a different output. The
machine will use some denumeration of all the machines. The
machine m' will go through the machines until it recognizes itself,
and then will use the universal machine m^* on the input (m,m') to
predict $m'(m)$. If the calculation of $m'(m)$ reaches a final state, it will
halt, but not before changing the output.

10.3 Is There a "Rational Player"?

We are ready to apply the previous section's results, taken from the
computability literature, into a game theoretic context. To recapitu-
late, our main goal in this chapter is to identify the bounds on
rationality emanating from the computability constraints. We will

focus on a two-player finite strategic game G; the scenario we have in mind is one where the input received by a machine is the description of the other machine, and the output of a player's machine determines the player's action.

Naively, one might say that in order to be "rational" in a game, player 1 has to first calculate the output of player 2's machine and then takes the best response to player 2's action. However, if player 2 does the same, namely, tries to calculate player 1's output, the calculation enters an infinite loop. It may be that a rational action can be arrived at differently, without player 1's machine first calculating player 2's choice. Because one machine gets the description of the other machine as input, it might be that a machine can calculate the best response in another fashion.

Discussing the question of rationality in a game where a player uses a machine to compute his action requires spelling out one more critical detail. Recall that a machine may never halt, or may halt with an output that does not match any of the alternatives. This creates a problem because the definition of a game requires that each player take an action. However, the standard model of a game does not specify any of the actions as a "default" action. Thus, we have to enrich the game model and to specify the action a player takes in case the machine does not halt or if it stops with an output that does not fit any of the available actions.

Henceforth, we adopt the assumption that each player i has one action, d_i, that is player i's default action. Whenever the machine does not produce a "legitimate" output, the player will play d_i. This is an arbitrary assumption. The need to adopt such an assumption demonstrates once again that the model of a game does not include details essential for including the deliberation phase within the analysis.

The results described in the previous section lead us to conclude that the existence of a rational player depends on the game to be played. Of course, if the game has a dominating strategy, a rational player does indeed exist. In less "obvious" games the existence of a rational player may also depend on the "default action."

In the Battle of the Sexes, if the default action of both players is b, then the machine m^*, described in Result 3, has the property that for any machine m, it yields an action that is a best response. It halts with the output a if and only if the other machine halts with the output a; it halts with the output b if $m(m^*)$ halts with the output b. In any case where $m(m^*)$ does not halt or produces a "faulty output" (output that is not the name of a strategy), $m^*(m)$ does the same and both play b.

The generalization of this argument is the following observation: Let G be a two-player strategic game with default actions d_1 and d_2 so that (d_1, d_2) is a Nash equilibrium. Then, each player i has a machine m_i^* so that for any machine m_j, the action resulting from $m_i^*(m_j)$ is a best response against the action resulting from $m_j(m_i^*)$.

Consider however the game

	a	b
a	3, 3	1, 2
b	1, 1	0, 0
c	0, 2	2, 0

with $d_i = b$ for both i. In order for m_1 to be a machine that always produces a best response, we need $m_1(m_2) = a$ if $m_2(m_1) = a$, and $m_1(m_2) = c$ whenever $m_2(m_1)$ either does not stop or stops with an output different from a (which may be either the action b or a faulty output). However, similar to Result 5, we can construct a machine m_2 that will confuse m_1: Whenever $m_1(m_2) = a$, it will produce $m_2(m_1) = b$, and whenever $m_1(m_2) = c$, the output $m_2(m_1)$ will be a. The machine m_1 will not produce a best response against machine m_2.

Thus, the existence of a machine that chooses for one player a best response to any machine of his opponent may not exist. In the

Battle of the Sexes with different default actions, there is no machine that calculates a best response to all opponents' possible machines, but when the two default actions coincide, such a machine exists.

In any case, I doubt that the nonexistence of a machine that is always "rational" validates the bounded rationality perspective. The simpler limitations on time, size of machine, and ability to make computations and observations drive the interesting difficulties encountered when using the rational man paradigm.

10.4 Turing Machine Game

Compare these three possible justifications for playing C in the Prisoner's Dilemma:

1. "I play C if and only if my opponent plays C."
2. "I play C because if I do not play C, my opponent will play D."
3. "I play C if and only if my opponent is like me."

The first two considerations seem to be problematic. The consideration, "I play C if and only if my opponent plays C," is not algorithmic and does not stipulate a unique action when the other player uses the same rule. The second consideration requires that each player knows the intentions of his opponent which depends on the player's action. The discussion in this section implies that nothing is "illogical" in consideration (3).

In the spirit of Chapters 8 and 9, for a given two-player game G we can define a machine game where each player i has to choose a machine m_i, which gets the description of the other player's machine, m_j, as an input, and selects the G-action $m_i(m_j)$. By choosing a machine, a player actually selects a response function to the machine chosen by his opponent. The response is not a response to the action taken but rather to the entire description of the opponent. In the previous section we considered rationality in the level of the

G-action; here we think about rationality in the machine game in the "machine-level."

Let G be the Prisoner's Dilemma. By Result 1, there is a machine m^* that plays C if and only if its opponent uses m^* as well. Thus, the pair of machines (m^*, m^*) is an equilibrium of the machine game that yields the G-outcome (C, C) even though the action D is the dominating action in the game G.

It is easy to generalize this observation to an arbitrary game, G. Recall the definition of an *enforceable* outcome of G used in Chapter 8: (a_1^*, a_2^*) is enforceable if, for each player i, there is an action of player j, p_j^* such that for all a_i, the outcome (p_j^*, a_i) is no better for player i than the outcome (a_1^*, a_2^*). One can show (see Project 2) that any enforceable outcome is an equilibrium outcome of the machine game.

10.5 Bibliographic Notes

From the many introductory books on computability, I strongly recommend Boolos and Jeffrey (1989) and Cutland (1980).

Many of the ideas in this chapter appeared in Binmore (1987) and Anderlini (1990). The presentation of the "self-recognizing" machine follows Howard (1988); see also McAfee (1984).

10.6 Projects

1. *Exercise* Build two Turing machines that will execute the operations of adding two natural numbers and of multiplying two natural numbers where the set of symbols on the tape includes only blanks and "1's" and a number n is represented by $n + 1$ successive 1's.

2. *Exercise* Explain the construction of two machines, m_1^* and m_2^*, that satisfy the condition that for each i, $m_i^*(m_j)$ always halts with the output x if $m_j = m_j^*$ and with the outcome y if $m_j \neq m_j^*$.

3. *Innovative* Analyze the "two drivers approaching a narrow bridge scenario" from the point of view of the analysis in this chapter.

4. *Innovative* Think about a game-theoretic setup in which Result 4 would be used.

5. *Reading* Read Anderlini and Felli (1994), which explores the extent to which incompleteness of contracts can be attributed to computability constraints. Form an opinion whether the computability constraints indeed explain the widespread existence of incomplete contracts.

6. *Reading* Read Rabin (1957) and explain the claim that "there are actual win-lose games that are strictly determined for which there is no effectively computable winning strategy."

11   Final Thoughts

11.1 Simon's Critique

At this stage, the reader may justifiably wonder about the place of
this book's subject within economic theory, and probably has critiques of the material presented. Herbert Simon, who was kind
enough to read a preliminary version of the book and to provide
me with comments, may have anticipated some of the reader's
critiques. As he puts it, he has "much to disagree with." I am sure
it would be useful for the reader, after reading the book, to listen
to the objections of the man who pioneered the field of "bounded
rationality." In the next section, I will take the opportunity to try to
respond to the critics by pointing out differences in our views about
"what economic theory is about."

Simon's objections can be summarized in three points.

1. The models discussed here originate from an "armchair position" and lack any empirical support, except for some reference to
the experiments by Tversky and Kahneman.

2. I ignore the huge body of literature, mainly in psychology and
artificial intelligence, that has succeeded in building models that fit
human behavior quite well.

3. Economics does not need more models. It should aim toward the discovery of principles to explain the many phenomena we observe empirically.

With Herbert Simon's kind permission, I will use his own words to elaborate. The following are excerpts from his letter, addressed to me, dated December 2, 1996.

Lack of Empirical Support

Referring to von Neumann and Morgenstern's *The Theory of Games and Economic Behavior*, Herbert Simon says: "Although I saw the great importance of the book, the lesson I drew from it was quite different, I think, from the lesson drawn by most game theorists. I concluded that the book's great contribution was to show that the whole concept of rationality became irremediably ill-defined when the possibility of outguessing was introduced, and that we must adopt some quite different framework and methodology to explain behavior under these conditions.

"Now I continue to have the same problem with the ingenious games that you describe in your lectures as I had with the original exposition of *n*-person games. Aside from the use you make of the Tversky-Kahneman experiments, for which I applaud you and them, almost the only reference to empirical matters that I detect in your pages is an occasional statements like "a casual observation" and "the phenomenon exhibited here is quite common."

"My training in science has installed in me a knee-jerk response to such statements. I ask automatically: 'How do you know'? 'What evidence can you provide to show that this is true'? Long experience in the natural sciences, both the more mathematized ones like physics and the more qualitative ones like biology, has shown that casual empiricism does not provide a firm foundation for the theories that fit the facts of the real world. Facts do not come from the armchair, but from careful observation and experimentation."

Neglecting the Literature

"In your opening chapter, you are very generous in crediting me with a major role in calling the attention of the economics profession to the need to introduce limits on human knowledge and computational ability into their models of rationality. (The idea, by the way, emerged not from speculation but from some very concrete observations I made on budgeting processes in the city government of Milwaukee.) But you seem to think that little has happened beyond the issuance of a manifesto, in the best tradition of a Mexican revolution. And you mainly propose more model building as the way to progress. You show no awareness of the vast amount of research (apart from the work of Tversky) that has been done (and mostly published in psychological and artificial intelligence journals) since the 1950s to provide empirical evidence about the phenomena of human decision making and problem solving (and thinking in general). Nor do you refer to cognitive psychology's considerable success in constructing theories from that evidence in the form of computer programs that demonstrably simulate in considerable detail . . . a wide range of both simple and complex human behaviors. Little of the behavior that has been studied is explicitly economic, but that provides no excuse for ignoring its relevance to economic analysis.

"Nor can it be objected that bodies of facts are useless without theoretical analysis, because most of these facts have now been embedded in (explained by?) fully formal theories that take the shape of computer programs (i.e., systems of non-numerical difference equations). For mathematicians, the unhappy detail is that these equations are almost never solvable in closed form, but must be explored with the help of simulation. But in this, we are no worse off than contemporary physicists."

Simon also provides recommended readings on the subject: "A non-technical introduction to this literature are Chapters 3 and 4 in

Simon (1996) and more technical treatments can be found in Simon (1979) and Newell and Simon (1972)."

Missing the Intention of the Profession

"Using the rubric of 'bounded rationality' to expand the arena of speculation misses the intent of my nagging of the economics profession. At the moment we don't need more models; we need evidence that will tell us what models are worth building and testing.

"So while I can get lots of fun, and good mathematical exercise, out of the rich collection of examples expounded in your lectures, I simply do not see how they lead to the kind of economic theory that we should all be seeking: a theory that describes real-world phenomena and begins to unify the description by the demonstration that a relatively small number of mechanisms (combined with a large body of knowledge about initial and boundary conditions) can produce all or most of these phenomena—not all of the phenomena that we can imagine, but those that actually occur."

11.2 Response

I will start by responding to what seems to me the most crucial criticism, "missing" the profession's intentions. I am aware of at least four different interpretations of economic theory:

1. Models of economic theory are aimed to predict behavior.

2. Models of economic theory are normative, in the sense that they are supposed to guide the economist in giving advice to economic agents about what to do.

3. Models of economic theory are exercises intended to sharpen economists' intuitions when dealing with complicated situations. Even if the models do not fully correspond to reality, dealing with such models is an indirect yet helpful activity.

4. Models of economic theory are meant to establish "linkages" between the concepts and statements that appear in our daily thinking on economic situations.

Herbert Simon has explicitly assumed the first two views while this book implicitly follows the fourth. By this approach, microeconomists are not prophets or consultants; neither are they educators of market agents. Economic models are viewed as being analogous to models in mathematical logic: Those models do not pretend to predict how people apply the values of truth to the statements of a natural language, or to provide instructions for their use; neither do they attempt to establish foundations for teaching "correct thinking." Analogously, by modeling bounded rationality, we try to examine the logic of a variety of principles that guide decision makers, especially within interactive systems (markets and games).

Thus, for example, from Hotelling's "main street" model, we learn that the desire to attain as large a share of the market as possible is a force that pushes vendors (or political parties, or the makers of soft drinks) toward positioning themselves or their products in the center. In real life, the many other motives that influence a vendor's choice will cause him sometimes not to be located at the center. It is nonetheless insightful to identify the exact logic that leads an economist to the conclusion that the desire to maximize the share of the market leads a vendor to be located at the center.

The crowning point of making microeconomic models is the discovery of simple and striking connections between concepts (and assertions) that initially appear remote. Consider, for example, the link, in the context of zero-sum games, between the maxmin principle and Nash equilibrium behavior; or between the core allocations and the competitive equilibrium allocations when the number of traders is "large."

The view of economic theory as an abstract discussion of models does not imply that the models are merely mathematical forms to be evaluated only by esthetics. In economic theory, we are interested in a model only if it refers to concepts and considerations that make sense in the context of social interactions. It is not that the model has to fit reality exactly. However, the basic components of the model have to be stated in a language that is close to the one actually in use. A model with this approach does not have to be verifiable in the way models in the sciences must be. Here, the test is not accomplished by feeding the variables with numbers and calculating predictions. The test lies in the ability to derive insights about the concepts dealt with.

In the context of "bounded rationality," we look for answers to questions like:

1. What are the relations between different kind of reasoning procedures?

2. To what extent are standard economic models sensitive to the existence of elements of bounded rationality?

3. Do procedural elements explain the existence of economic institutions?

Note that this list is different from what Simon suggests as the "Bounded Rationality" questions. In a letter dated February 7, 1997, Simon says: "In my version of bounded rationality we look for answers to questions like:

1. What are the kinds of reasoning procedures that people actually use, and why (in terms of knowledge of their psychological makeup)? What are the effects of social environment and social history on the procedures used? To what extent are other procedures usable? In what ways does the introduction of computers into business change these procedures?

2. What are the economic consequences of their using these procedures and not others? In what respects are current economic models deficient in the assumptions they make about reasoning procedures?

3. In terms of what psychological and social mechanisms can the existence and structure of economic institutions be explained?"

Let me go back to the first of Herbert Simon's criticisms: the lack of empirical evidence to support the assumptions about individuals' behavior. Under the approach that views our investigation as an inquiry into the "logic of procedural rationality and of the interaction between procedurally rational agents," the test of relevance is simply the naturalness of the concepts which we study and the ability to derive, by their use, interesting analytical conclusions. Thus, the satisficing procedure of Simon is an interesting concept, not because it was empirically shown to be popular but because it sounds like a reasonable ingredient of our decision making. This by itself justifies those beautiful studies that draw analytical connections between, for instance, the satisficing criterion and optimization when taking search costs into account.

The issue is analogous to the question as to whether we need empirical evidence to support philosophical investigations. Philosophers usually do not make empirical or experimental inquiries about the contents of the notions (such as "rational," "good," and "fair") they investigate, although they do bring forth arguments based on the way these concepts are used in practice.

Overall, I agree with Herbert Simon that the departures from the rational man paradigm have to be based on some empirical (or experimental) observations about the basic motives that drive decision makers. The number of deviations from a fully "rational" model is so large that we must content ourselves with the study of extensions that make more sense. This underlies the relevance of some of the cognitive psychological literature, especially work that explicates the clear and simple motives that often appear in real decision making. For the purpose of the analysis we are making here, however, we need only confirmation of our speculations about the basic ingredients; we do not require detailed, complicated models of the type that the artificial intelligence literature provides.

Here, I have neglected this very interesting literature not only because of my ignorance, and not solely due to considerations related to confining myself to the type of methods I have used, but also because those models do not share a methodological tradition with this book. Those models may be capable of producing imitations of human behavior, but they are not convenient components for analytical work.

The economics profession has several legitimate tasks. Not all economists seek the same goals. The literature surveyed here does not pretend to predict or advise. The models are perceived as patterns of views adopted about the world. Given such an approach, the most one can do is to clarify the concepts we use. But I do hope that scholars in the field, and especially students, have found within this book ideas to be more deeply pursued.

References

Abreu, D., and A. Rubinstein. (1988). "The Structure of Nash Equilibrium in Repeated Games with Finite Automata." *Econometrica* 56, 1259–1282.

Anderson, J. R. (1983). *The Architecture of Cognition.* Cambridge, Mass.: Harvard University Press.

Anderlini, L. (1990). "Some Notes on Church's Thesis and the Theory of Games." *Theory and Decision* 29, 15–52.

Anderlini, L., and L. Felli. (1994). "Incomplete Written Contracts: Undescribable States of Nature." *Quarterly Journal of Economics* 109, 1086–1124.

Arrow, K. J. (1987). "Rationality of Self and Others in an Economic System." In R. M. Hogarth and M. W. Reder, eds. *Rational Choice: The Contrast Between Economics and Psychology,* 201–216. Chicago: University of Chicago Press.

Aumann, R. (1976). "Agreeing to Disagree." *The Annals of Statistics* 4, 1236–1239.

Aumann, R. (1996). "Rationality and Bounded Rationality." Nancy Schwartz Lecture, Kellogg Foundation.

Azipurua, J. M., T. Ichiishi, J. Nieto, and J. R. Uriarte. (1993). "Similarity and Preferences in the Space of Simple Lotteries." *Journal of Risk and Uncertainty* 6, 289–297.

Banks, J., and R. Sundaram. (1990). "Repeated Games, Finite Automata, and Complexity." *Games and Economic Behavior* 2, 97–117.

Bartholdi, J. J., C. A. Tovey, and M. A. Trick. (1989). "The Computational Difficulty of Manipulating an Election." *Social Choice and Welfare* 6, 227–241.

Benartzi, S., and R. Thaler. (1995). "Myopic Loss Aversion and the Equity Premium Puzzle." *Quarterly Journal of Economics* 110, 73–92.

Ben-Porath, E. (1993). "Repeated Games with Finite Automata." *Journal of Economic Theory* 59, 17–32.

Binmore, K. (1987). "Modeling Rational Players, I." *Economics and Philosophy* 3, 179–214.

Binmore, K. (1988). "Modeling Rational Players, II." *Economics and Philosophy* 4, 9–55.

Boolos, G. S., and R. C. Jeffrey. (1989). *Computability and Logic*. Third edition. New York: Cambridge University Press.

Camerer, C. (1994). "Individual Decision Making." In J. Kagel and A. Roth, eds. *Handbook of Experimental Economics*, 587–704. Princeton, N.J.: Princeton University Press.

Chatterjee, K., and H. Sabourian. (1996). "Multiperson Bargaining and Strategic Complexity." Mimeo.

Chen, H-C., J. W. Friedman, and J.-F. Thisse. (1997). "Boundedly Rational Nash Equilibrium: A Probabilistic Choice Approach." *Games and Economic Behavior* 18, 32–54.

Cho, I-K. (1995). "Perceptrons Play the Repeated Prisoner's Dilemma." *Journal of Economic Theory* 67, 266–284.

Cutland, N. J. (1980). *Computability*. New York: Cambridge University Press.

Derman, C. (1970). *Finite State Markovian Decision Processes*. New York: Academic Press.

Dow, J. (1991). "Search Decisions with Limited Memory." *Review of Economic Studies* 58, 1–14.

Elster, J. (1979). *Ulysses and the Sirens: Studies in Rationality and Irrationality*. New York: Cambridge University Press.

Fagin, R., J. Halpern, Y. Moses, and M. Vardi. (1995). *Reasoning About Knowledge*. Cambridge, Mass.: MIT Press.

Fershtman, C., and E. Kalai. (1993). "Complexity Considerations and Market Behavior." *Rand Journal of Economics* 24, 224–235.

Geanakoplos, J. (1989). "Game Theory Without Partitions, and Applications To Speculation and Consensus." *Journal of Economic Theory*.

Geanakoplos, J. (1992). "Common Knowledge, Bayesean Learning and Market Speculation with Bounded Rationality." *Journal of Economic Perspectives* 6, 58–82.

Geanakoplos, J. (1994). "Common Knowledge." In R. Aumann and S. Hart, eds. *Handbook of Game Theory*, 1438–1496. Leiden: Elsevier.

Gilboa, I., and D. Schmeidler. (1995). "Case-based Decision Theory." *Quarterly Journal of Economics* 110, 605–639.

Gilboa, I., and D. Schmeidler. (1997). "Act Similarity in Case-based Decision Theory." *Economic Theory* 9, 47–61.

Hendon, E., J. Jacobsen, and B. Sloth. (1996). "The One-Shot-Deviation Principle for Sequential Rationality." *Games and Economic Behavior* 12, 274–282.

Hintikka, J. (1962). *Knowledge and Belief*. Ithaca, N.Y.: Cornell University Press.

Hogarth, R. M., and M. W. Reder, eds. (1987). *Rational Choice: The Contrast Between Economics and Psychology*. Chicago: University of Chicago Press.

Hopcroft, J. E., and J. D. Ullman. (1979). *Introduction to Automata Theory: Languages and Computation*. Reading, Mass.: Addison Wesley.

Howard, J. (1988). "Cooperation in the Prisoner's Dilemma." *Theory and Decision* 24, 203–213.

Huber, J., J. Payne, and C. Puto. (1982). "Adding Asymmetrically Dominated Alternatives: Violations of Regularity and the Similarity Hypothesis." *Journal of Consumer Research* 9, 90–98.

Isbell, J. (1957). "Finitary Games." In D. Dresher, A. W. Tucker, and P. Wolfe, eds. *Contributions to the Theory of Games* III, 79–96. Princeton, N.J.: Princeton University Press.

Jehiel, P. (1995). "Limited Forecast in Repeated Alternate Games." *Journal of Economic Behavior* 67, 497–519.

Kahneman, D., and A. Tversky. (1982). "Prospect Theory: An Analysis of Decision Under Risk." *Econometrica* 24, 178–191.

Kreps, D. M. (1988). *Notes on the Theory of Choice*. Boulder, Colo.: Westview Press.

Kreps, D. M., P. Milgrom, J. Roberts, and R. Wilson. (1982). "Rational Cooperation in the Finitely Repeated Prisoner's Dilemma." *Journal of Economic Theory* 27, 245–252.

Kuhn, H. W. (1953). "Extensive Games and the Problem of Information." In D. Dresher, A. W. Tucker, and P. Wolfe, eds. *Contributions to the Theory of Games* II, 193–216. Princeton, N.J.: Princeton University Press.

Lewis, D. (1969). *Convention: A Philosophical Study*. Cambridge, Mass.: Harvard University Press.

Lipman, B. (1995a). "Information Processing and Bounded Rationality: A Survey." *Canadian Journal of Economics* 28, 42–67.

Lipman, B. (1995b). "Decision Theory Without Logical Omniscience: Toward an Axiomatic Framework for Bounded Rationality." Mimeo.

Luce, R. D. (1956). "Semiorders and a Theory of Utility Discrimination." *Econometrica* 24, 178–191.

Luce, R. D. (1959). *Individual Choice Behavior: A Theoretical Analysis.* New York: John Wiley.

Luce, R. D., and H. Raiffa. (1957). *Games and Decisions.* New York: John Wiley.

Marschak, J., and R. Radner. (1972). *Economic Theory of Teams.* New Haven, Conn.: Yale University Press.

Matsui, A. (1994). "Expected Utility and Case-based Reasoning." Mimeo.

McAfee, R. P. (1984). "Effective Computability in Economic Decisions." Mimeo.

McKelvey, R. D., and T. R. Palfrey. (1995). "Quantal Response Equilibria for Normal Form Games." *Games and Economic Behavior* 10, 6–38.

Meyer, M. (1991). "Learning from Coarse Information: Biased Contests and Career Profiles." *Review of Economic Studies* 58, 15–41.

Milgrom, P., and N. Stokey. (1982). "Information, Trade and Common Knowledge." *Journal of Economic Theory* 26, 17–27.

Minsky, M. L., and S. A. Papert. (1988). *Perceptrons.* Cambridge, Mass.: MIT Press.

Neme, A., and L. Quintas. (1990). "Subgame Perfect Equilibria of Repeated Games with Cost of Implementation." *Journal of Economic Theory* 58, 105–109.

Ng, Y. K. (1977). "Bentham or Bergson? Finite Sensitivity, Utility Functions and Social Welfare Function." *Review of Economic Studies* 44, 545–569.

Newell, A., and H. Simon. (1972). *Human Problem Solving.* Englewood Cliffs, N.J.: Prentice-Hall.

Neyman, A. (1985). "Bounded Complexity Justifies Cooperation in the Finitely Repeated Prisoner's Dilemma." *Economics Letters* 19, 227–229.

Osborne, M., and A. Rubinstein. (1994). *A Course in Game Theory.* Cambridge, Mass.: MIT Press.

Osborne, M., and A. Rubinstein. (1997). "Games with Procedurally Rational Players." *American Economic Review* (forthcoming).

Payne, J.W., J. R. Battman, and E. J. Johnson. (1988). "Adaptive Strategy Selection in Decision Making." *Journal of Experimental Psychology: Learning, Memory and Cognition* 14, 534–552.

Piccione, M. (1992). "Finite Automata Equilibria with Discounting." *Journal of Economic Theory* 56, 180–193.

Piccione, M., and A. Rubinstein. (1993). "Finite Automata Play a Repeated Extensive Game." *Journal of Economic Theory* 61, 160–168.

Piccione, M., and A. Rubinstein. (1997). "On the Interpretation of Decision Problems with Imperfect Recall." *Games and Economic Behavior* 20, 3–24.

Rabin, M. O. (1957). "Effective Computability of Winning Strategies." In D. Dresher, A. W. Tucker, and P. Wolfe, eds. *Contributions to the Theory of Games* III, 147–157. Princeton, N. J.: Princeton University Press.

Radner, R. (1986). "Can Bounded Rationality Resolve the Prisoner's Dilemma?" In A. Mas-Colell and W. Hildenbrand, eds. *Essays in Honor of Gerard Debreu*, 387–399. Amsterdam: North-Holland.

Radner, R. (1992). "Hierarchy: The Economics of Managing." *Journal of Economic Literature* 30, 1382–1415.

Radner, R. (1993). "The Organization of Decentralized Information Processing." *Econometrica* 61, 1109–1146.

Rosenthal, R. (1982). "Games of Perfect Information, Predatory Pricing and the Chain-Store Paradox." *Journal of Economic Theory* 25, 92–100.

Rosenthal, R. (1989). "A Bounded-Rationality Approach to the Study of Noncooperative Games." *International Journal of Game Theory* 18, 273–292.

Rosenthal, R. (1993). "Rules of Thumb in Games." *Journal of Economic Behavior and Organization* 22, 1–13.

Rubinstein, A. (1986). "Finite Automata Play a Repeated Prisoner's Dilemma" *Journal of Economic Theory* 39, 83–96.

Rubinstein, A. (1987). "Is There a 'Finite Automata' Resolution to the Finitely Repeated Games Paradoxes?" Mimeo.

Rubinstein, A. (1988). "Similarity and Decision-Making Under Risk." *Journal of Economic Theory* 46, 145–153.

Rubinstein, A. (1990). "New Directions in Economic Theory—Bounded Rationality." *Revista Española de Economía* 7, 3–15.

Rubinstein, A. (1991). "Comments on the Interpretation of Game Theory." *Econometrica* 59, 909–924.

Rubinstein, A. (1993). "On Price Recognition and Computational Complexity in a Monopolistic Model." *Journal of Political Economy* 101, 473–484.

Rubinstein, A., and A. Wolinsky. (1990). "On the Logic of 'Agreeing to Disagree' Type Results." *Journal of Economic Theory* 51, 184–193.

Salop, S. (1977). "The Noisy Monopolist: Imperfect Information, Price Dispersion and Price Discrimination." *Review of Economic Studies* 44, 393–406.

Selten, R. (1978). "The Chain Store Paradox." *Theory and Decision* 9, 127–159.

Selten, R. (1989). "Evolution, Learning, and Economic Behavior." Nancy Schwartz Lecture, Kellogg Foundation.

Shafir, E., P. Diamond, and A. Tversky. (1997). "Money Illusion." *Quarterly Journal of Economics,* in press.

Shafir, E., and A. Tversky. (1995). "Decision Making." In D. N. Osherson and E. E. Smith, eds. *Invitation to Cognitive Science: Thinking,* 77–109. Cambridge, Mass.: MIT Press.

Shafir, E., I. Simonson, and A. Tversky. (1993). "Reason-Based Choice." *Cognition* 49, 11–36.

Simon, H. A. (1955). "A Behavioral Model of Rational Choice." *Quarterly Journal of Economics* 69, 99–118.

Simon, H. A. (1956). "Rational Choice and the Structure of the Environment." *Psychological Review* 63, 129–138.

Simon, H. A. (1972). "Theories of Bounded Rationality." In C. B. McGuire and R. Radner, eds. *Decision and Organization,* 161–176. Amsterdam: North Holland.

Simon, H. A. (1976). "From Substantive to Procedural Rationality." In S. J. Latis, ed. *Methods and Appraisal in Economics,* 129–148. New York: Cambridge University Press.

Simon, H. A. (1979). *Models of Thought.* New Haven, Conn.: Yale University Press.

Simon, H. A. (1982). *Models of Bounded Rationality,* volume 2. Cambridge, Mass.: MIT Press.

Simon, H. A. (1996). *The Sciences of the Artificial.* Third edition. Cambridge, Mass.: MIT Press.

Simonson, I. (1989). "Choice Based on Reasons: The Case of Attraction and Compromise Effects." *Journal of Consumer Research* 16, 158–174.

Strotz, R. H. (1956). "Myopia and Inconsistency in Dynamic Utility Maximization." *Review of Economic Studies* 23, 165–180.

Thompson, F. B. (1952). "Equivalence of Games in Extensive Form." Rand Corporation Research Memorandum RM-759. Reprinted in *Classics in Game Theory.* (1997). H. W. Kuhn (ed.) Princeton: Princeton University Press.

Tversky, A. (1969). "Intransitivities of Preferences." *Psychological Review* 76, 31–48.

Tversky, A. (1977). "Features of Similarity." *Psychological Review* 84, 327–352.

Tversky, A., and D. Kahneman. (1981). "The Framing of Decisions and the Psychology of Choice." *Science* 211, 453–458.

Tversky, A., and D. Kahneman. (1986). "Rational Choice and the Framing of Decisions." *Journal of Business* 59, 251–278.

Tversky, A., and E. Shafir. (1992). "Choice Under Conflict: The Dynamics of the Deferred Decision." *Psychological Science* 3, 358–361.

Van Zandt, T. (1996). "Hidden Information Acquisition and Static Choice." *Theory and Decision* 40, 235–247.

Varian, H. (1972). "Complexity of Social Decisions." Mimeo.

Watanabe, S. (1969). *Knowing and Guessing*. New York: John Wiley.

Yampuler, E. (1995). "A Principal with Bounded Complexity Optimality Deduces Information by Designing a Mechanism with Free-choice Disclosure." Mimeo.

Zemel, E. (1989). "Small Talk and Cooperation: A Note on Bounded Rationality." *Journal of Economic Theory* 49, 1–9.

Index